I Remember Nelson Mandela

I Remember Nelson Mandela

Edited by
Vimla Naidoo & Sahm Venter

'Nothing is more important than to be loved by your colleagues.'

— Nelson Mandela, 5 August 2008, addressing the staff of the Nelson Mandela Foundation at a private celebration for his 90th birthday

First published by Jacana Media (Pty) Ltd, in association with the Nelson Mandela Foundation, in 2018

10 Orange Street
Sunnyside
Auckland Park 2092
South Africa
+2711 628 3200
www.jacana.co.za

© Individual contributors, 2018
© Cover image: George Hallett

All rights reserved.

ISBN 978-1-4314-2662-1

Cover design by publicide
Editing by Megan Mance
Proofreading by Lara Jacob
Set in MrsEaves 11.5/14pt
Printed and bound by CTP Printers, Cape Town
Job no. 003272

See a complete list of Jacana titles at www.jacana.co.za

Dedicated to the scores of women and men who served Nelson Mandela in various capacities from the time he was released from prison, through his presidency and his retirement. Their commitment and care provided Madiba with valued support in his work and life.

Foreword

One of Madiba's great gifts was that he never took anyone for granted and he valued every single person who came across his path. In particular, he held a deep appreciation for his dedicated staff, whether they worked in our household, his office, in his security team or, at the end, in his medical team.

Their presence in his life touched him as a human being, and all the tasks they performed allowed him the space to focus on the demands of his extraordinary calling. They made his daily life easier and freed him to meet his bigger obligations. He truly treasured each person who worked for him, which is why he always made the time to say to them, 'Good morning. How are you?' He was genuinely concerned about their wellbeing. He would ask them about their loved ones and often supported them to resolve their own family issues.

It is precisely because I witnessed his thoughtfulness and concern for those who worked for him that, after his passing, I felt I should meet with as many of them as possible to express my gratitude and say 'thank you'. I had to express my appreciation in my own right because they made my life, as his wife, much easier as well. I convened them for touching reflection sessions on their time working for Madiba and thanked them on behalf of the two of us. We, as Africans, believe that wherever you are in the world, when you experience a loss, if you do not have a chance to look closely into a person's eyes, there can be no closure. I would not have had peace with myself if I had not met with them, mourned the loss of our beloved Madiba together, and thanked them sincerely for their service.

Most of the people who have contributed their stories to this book were part of our lives for many years. They took care of Madiba and me, and helped raise our grandchildren. They became like family to us. We went through so much together — beautiful moments and difficult moments. Therefore, it was important for me to meet face to face with each of them, and to experience the closure of his passing in a space of gratitude and love.

The idea to gather the memories of those who served Madiba into a book came from an understanding that most people in South Africa, and those around the world, knew him as an icon; as a public figure. It was important to me that the stories of those close to him be published so that fifty years from now, even a hundred years from now, when future generations want to know who Nelson Mandela was, they would not only be told the story of the head of state, but they would be able to read the story of a human being with a caring heart and generous soul.

Many people have their own stories of what Madiba meant to them, but the people in this book are those who occupied a significant place in his life from the time he came out of jail. They may have even spent more time with him than his own family. They travelled everywhere with him and grew to know him on a personal level. Their unique and intimate stories need to be heard.

It is critical for me that the individual members of the teams who supported Madiba in their different capacities are not wiped out of our history, but that they are acknowledged for what they did for him. For me, the best recognition we could give to them was this opportunity to tell their touching stories.

Now that this book has finally been completed it will give a name to these women and men who shared so much with Madiba. It will give them a face and it will give them a voice. I want people who read these stories to see Madiba through the eyes of his staff. Even when he was President, Madiba did not lose sight of his own humanity. His human side could easily be forgotten if we had not created this space for people to share their memorable experiences with him in his everyday life.

I would like to thank the Nelson Mandela Foundation for accepting as a duty my idea to create this book. Particularly, I would like to thank Vimla Naidoo and Sahm Venter for collecting all these memories and curating them here. I would also like to thank those who took up the challenge and shared their heart-warming stories for the world to now enjoy.

For me personally this book is a significant record of history and I am happy to have this collection of tributes to Madiba from those who provided him with comfort and security, and often made him smile. He connected with them in a very special way and it is imperative to me that they are recognised for their important contributions to his life.

Graça Machel
2018

A Note from the Editors

Nelson Mandela was supported by the service of a cast of hundreds. In this, the year of the centenary of his birth, we present this collection of memories from more than one hundred people about working for Madiba. Laced together these quirky, poignant and humorous recollections evoke the Madiba they saw at close range and often out of the public eye.

Our thanks must first go to Graça Machel, known as 'Mum' by the staff, whose vision this book was back in 2014.

We could not reach everyone who worked with Madiba from his release from prison in 1990 until his passing in 2013. Some had themselves passed on and are represented here in the 'In Memoriam' section by seven people who were important to Madiba. For their permission to publish their words we appreciate the family of Professor Jakes Gerwel and the Jakes Gerwel Family Trust, Barbara Hogan, Fikile Masikane, Nkuleleko Mtwazi, George Mxadana, Annemarie de Greef and the Sisulu family. Special thanks to Professor John Higgins for allowing us to use extracts from 'Living out our differences: Reflections on Mandela, Marx and my country: An interview with Jakes Gerwel'.

Still others could not be traced, and a few declined, believing their stories not to be interesting enough.

The memories from women and men in South Africa and in seven other countries represent all those who share the honour of having helped one of the greatest human beings the world has known. Their contributions have been placed generally in the order in which they first began working with Madiba to maintain a broad chronology of events.

We are deeply grateful to each of the contributors whose words sparked in us other memories, like the rally in Khayelitsha when Madiba stopped his speech, pointed a finger towards the crowd of a hundred thousand people and spoke sternly into the microphone: 'You! Don't talk when I am talking.'

Not only were they generous with their memories, they also connected us with their former colleagues. In this regard, we particularly appreciate the efforts of Ashwyn Govind, Fuad Floris, Zelda la Grange and Tony Trew. Ben Harris went above and beyond.

Thanks to Sello Hatang and Verne Harris for supporting this project and the staff of the Nelson Mandela Foundation, some of whom contributed their memories. Thank you to our publishers Maggie Davey, Bridget Impey and Sibongile Machika for believing in this book. To Megan Mance, Lara Jacob, Shay Heydenrych, Nadia Goetham, Russell Starke, Stavi Kotsiovos, Shawn Paikin, Tarryn Talbot, Neilwe Mashigo, Lutendo Mabata and the rest of the team at Jacana. Thanks also to Mark

Govender, Claude Colart and the late Libby Lloyd for their encouragement.

Gratitude is also due to Denis Hirson, whose own book, *I Remember King Kong (The Boxer)* revived George Perec's elegant style of reminiscences and inspired the form of this book.

Vimla Naidoo & Sahm Venter
2018

Mac Maharaj

I REMEMBER the occasion when, against my better judgement, Madiba made me dress in a 'penguin suit' – the white dress shirt, black bow tie, tail coat and pinstriped pants. As President of South Africa he was on a state visit to the United Kingdom. At the hotel Zelda advised us that an outfitter would call to dress us in hired suits for the banquet where Madiba would host the Queen. 'Oh, no!' I objected. I was not going to be turned into a penguin. A revolutionary kitted in a penguin suit! In deference to the Queen, *nogal*! 'Orders of the President,' was Zelda's unyielding retort. I was a member of the Cabinet, there to serve my country at the pleasure of the President. The next evening there we were, all members of his delegation, every one of us waddled into the banquet hall looking like penguins lost in the Kalahari.

I REMEMBER that the Queen was splendidly regal in her outfit. And there was Madiba, not in a penguin suit, but in black pants and a loose black silk shirt. I guess he chuckled to himself all evening as he looked down from the main table at his discomforted penguins while he relaxed in his cool outfit.

I REMEMBER that it took me back to our prison days when Madiba advised me to learn to exercise self-control and put a dampener on my temper. I was continually getting into hot water with the Robben Island authorities. He urged me, 'Pause. Make sure your retorts to the warders are carefully worded. Cut to the quick like a scalpel. Don't just blunder your way by using abusive words that they will use against you. Count to ten. If needs be, pretend you are angry. Control your anger. Don't let anger control your conduct and words.' It helped me steer through many difficult moments. It still does, though I now am never certain when I am simulating anger and when I am truly consumed with fury.

I REMEMBER how he enabled me to understand that leadership is more about how you conduct yourself than about the rhythm and rhyme of mesmerising words. Surrounded by baton-wielding warders, our column of prisoners was marched to work at the lime quarry, with warders demanding that we trot, rather than walk. From somewhere within the column came the whispered words among us to walk slowly. I was on the flank of the column and in the direct line of the warders' blows. It was all very well for Madiba to give that advice from the safety of the body of the column! I reckoned he would sing a different tune if he were as close to the batons as I was. My mind wanted to follow his advice while my legs seemed to listen to the warders.

I REMEMBER how he wended his way unobtrusively from the bosom of the column to the front row, where, by force of example, he slowed us all down. Silently and in unison we went into slow mode. Their threats became hollow; their power rendered powerless.

I REMEMBER that on that day he demonstrated that leadership is earned; that it is not what one thinks of oneself; it is how others — friends and foes — see you. I try to live by that experience, though I have to admit that from time to time I fail myself. When I remember the ambling pace set by Madiba I am reminded that actions speak louder than words and unity in action can help us scale unclimbable mountains.

I REMEMBER how, in that cold and soul-deadening loneliness of the prison cell, he wrapped his pain in a blanket, sat motionless and expressionless, when he learnt on different occasions of the death of his mother, of the passing of his son Thembi, and of the torture that comrade Winnie was subjected to in detention without trial.

I REMEMBER those moments because, while many know of the brutalities — both physical and psychological — that we detainees and prisoners experienced and admire us for surviving, few know that the greater pain we underwent was the agony, suffering and torture of our families outside — our parents, spouses and children.

I REMEMBER because, no matter the torture I bore in detention in 1964, it was the assault in detention of my wife Tim by Warrant Officer Erasmus that I could not endure. It was a different kind of pain compounded by a searing sense of helplessness. It turned forever the iron in my soul into steel.

I REMEMBER a rare moment when Madiba almost assaulted a warder for denigrating his wife, Winnie.

I REMEMBER those moments of pain and helplessness that were visited upon Madiba and understood how they planted within us an everlasting sense of guilt that we failed our families when they needed us the most; that the honour of serving the cause of freedom belongs to them. When shall we bring their deeds out of the shadows, to shine the light on them?

Jason Tshabalala

I REMEMBER Madiba being very disciplined. One of his grandsons came home and when Madiba asked him how school was he said he had lost part of his uniform. Madiba said, 'No, this is not acceptable.' So what he did was he took him and he made him stand in the garden holding a blanket as a punishment, for almost an hour. I saw him just standing there with his arms out holding this blanket. I asked, 'What happened?' And he said, 'Uncle Jason, Grandad is punishing me because I lost my uniform.'

I REMEMBER when Madiba went to see a doctor for his annual medical examination. After they took blood they put a plaster on his arm so he wouldn't bleed. I think when he was washing his hands he accidentally removed the plaster and he started bleeding.

I REMEMBER him shouting, 'Jason! Jason! Come inside!' So I went into the bathroom and he said, 'Can you tell the doctor that I'm bleeding!' He was quite scared. I said, 'We have to just go back and they must put a bandage over it.'

I REMEMBER that as a leader Madiba was not afraid to go to difficult areas that were affected by violence. We went all over the country – KZN, the East Rand, to the different sites — and for us it was a bit of a challenge to ensure his safety, which was of paramount importance for us. But at the same time we needed to give him the space to be able to visit the victims.

I REMEMBER after the Boipatong Massacre we went to the Vaal and from there we went to the Sharpeville Stadium where there was a rally. People were justifiably angry and it was very tense in the stadium. Madiba was trying to calm the people and they started singing, 'We want weapons. We want firearms.'

I REMEMBER that in the midst of that anger Madiba said, 'We mustn't behave like the apartheid government. The ANC has suspended the armed struggle and we have to ensure that we don't carry out revenge attacks.' He was able to encourage the people to focus and be calm to ensure the continuation of the negotiations to end white minority rule.

I REMEMBER his remarkable bravery in going to areas that were no-go zones. We once went to Ngwelezane in northern Natal where there was a lot of violence. The ANC leadership asked him to go and visit the houses that had been burnt there. We were against him going and we advised the leadership that we couldn't go there. But Madiba insisted. We tried to persuade him but he said, 'No no no no, your job is to protect me. It's not to tell me where not to go.' We came out of the cars to inspect some of the houses and at the second house shots were fired in our direction. We just put him in the car and we evacuated the area.

I REMEMBER when we were flying in a two-engine propeller plane from Lanseria Airport to Pietermaritzburg for the election campaign. Just before we landed there was a technical problem with one of the engines and you could hear the sound. The plane took a slight dive and Madiba said, 'Do you think everything is okay? Can I speak to the pilot?' So one of the pilots came out and said, 'Everything is okay, Mr President.' I was on the radio with the guys on the ground and they told me that they had dispatched the emergency services. There was obviously something wrong. I couldn't tell Madiba. I laughed because he said to the people in the plane, 'You know, these pilots will never tell you the truth even if you are in trouble.' He had a sense of humour even in the face of an emergency.

Andile Ngxabani

I REMEMBER when we were working with Madiba as protectors we had to expect the unexpected. You must not only concentrate on the security. You must open your mind, anything can happen.

I REMEMBER that Madiba was very serious about security but when he saw children playing he would stop the convoy so he could go and greet the children. We were not supposed to do that but we had to do it for him.

I REMEMBER that when we were planning his route and we knew he would probably pass children we would warn our colleagues, 'Guys on the left hand side there are children. Take care, we might stop.'

I REMEMBER him getting out of his car and going to children who were playing soccer in a field. They were aged around eight, nine, ten. Sometimes they wouldn't know who he was and when we told them they became so excited. We would have to line them up because they would be jumping around.

I REMEMBER that he would ask them how they are and laugh with them and remember the rhymes we learnt when we were young. He would sing with them, 'Baa Baa Black Sheep, have you any wool?'

I REMEMBER when Madiba was replacing mud structures for properly built schools and clinics in the Transkei area. He used to take business people from Johannesburg in his plane to a place identified for a school and then he would say to them, 'Can a human being grow in a place like this?' And that's all that he would say. He wouldn't say 'build this, build that'. He would say, 'I don't want any money from you, these are the people of the area, just interact with them.'

I REMEMBER when he went on his walks around the bundus of Qunu he didn't want to be seen with a vehicle. When people were taking their sheep to the field, he wanted to meet them, greet them. But anything could have happened so we always needed to be proactive and bring a vehicle. Although he was a great and respected man, wherever he was he wanted to be with the people.

Jeremy Vearey

I REMEMBER in 1990 shortly after my release from Robben Island prison, Comrades Wally Rhoode, David Fortuin and twelve others had the privilege of being trained by the British Special Air Services (SAS) unit as personal bodyguards for Nelson Mandela.

I REMEMBER that after the blood and sweat of the SAS course we were unexpectedly honoured by the presence of Madiba himself. This iconic leader for whom I would have taken a bullet called me by my name and asked me about the health of my grandmother who I was taking care of.

I REMEMBER in December 1993, working as Madiba's bodyguard on a well-deserved holiday in the Bahamas. During one of his morning walks I noticed that he was cross with me. After an uncomfortable silence he asked me why I hadn't told him that my grandmother had died and that she had been buried two days before.

I REMEMBER Madiba deciding that we should go to Beaufort West before the 1994 elections despite information that the AWB under the command of a certain 'Colonel' Munroe would block the town with his 'soldiers' and occupy the hotel with his 'Iron Guard'. As we had predicted when we arrived with Tata and heavily armed ANC security and intelligence agents, we were faced with the reality of the AWB blockade. But they had not taken into account the power of the ordinary people of Beaufort West who fearlessly positioned themselves next to us at the hotel where Tata was staying. We told all the AWB people there that if anything happened to Tata they would not get out alive.

I REMEMBER the real lesson in leadership that day was demonstrated by Tata's decision to talk to 'Colonel' Munroe after weapons were dropped. One of the Iron Guard members objected, saying that the whole time I had my weapon trained on him. 'Colonel' Munroe then asked if that is how Tata's people received the AWB leadership. Tata asked me to lower my weapon but told Munroe that there were thousands like me who would fight the AWB. It was then that Munroe asked to be excused and hastily left the town with his Iron Guard and AWB commandos. Tata's lesson in leadership was straight from our revolutionary philosophy that anyone can be a selfless and unbreakable shield for our freedom.

Fuad Floris

I REMEMBER when we were in the Transkei we often used Oryx helicopters to fly around because it took a strain on the Old Man to drive to visit his cousins, the Matanzimas. We were returning from Cofimvaba with this Oryx and Madiba asked if the pilot knew where a particular king lived. One of the pilots who was on board was the one who had taken him to the king on a previous occasion so he could remember the GPS readings and where to land the aircraft. It was completely unplanned; the President of the country, like a passenger asking an Uber driver just to change direction, without planning or anything. Nothing was planned on the ground, we were going to land, but we didn't know what we were going to do when we arrived. The chopper landed on a field and the Old Man got out and he started to walk. He walked onto the road and he stopped the first bakkie that came along, it was a decrepit bakkie that was almost falling apart.

I REMEMBER that he talked to the driver and the driver said he was welcome to get in. Madiba battled to close the door because it was almost falling apart. Some of us jumped onto the bakkie, others ran at the sides of the bakkie to visit the king. What I found unusual was that the President of the country would get into an old bakkie and sit and chat with the driver while the security guys are on the bakkie and some are running on the sides.

I REMEMBER we were in Brixton in London when the crowd jumped over the barriers and blocked the road to get to see Madiba. Our convoy couldn't drive because of the amount of people in the road and it was only the Rolls Royce with Prince Charles and the Old Man that could drive slowly through the crowd. There were policemen with horses and this special escort group, called the SEG – smart guys with brand new BMW motorbikes all in their leather tunics driving in front and us security people ran the fenders to get out of the crowd as we normally do. We ran for at least a kilometre. But there was no transport for us because the other part of the convoy was stuck behind and the only transport available was these motorcycles. In Britain you are not allowed on a motorcycle without a helmet and there we were on these motorcycles in the heart of London, in Brixton with our ties blowing in the wind.

I REMEMBER how we lost Madiba. When the driver eventually realised that he had left the rest of the convoy behind he drove to a police station but obviously these other guys didn't know where the Rolls Royce with Madiba and Prince Charles was. I think they went to the Kensington Police Station. It was possible that they communicated somehow through a control point. So the rest of the convoy had to join us at the police station and then from there go back to the hotel. It was very unusual for the Prince to rock up at the police station with Nelson Mandela out of the blue without any plan or anything.

I REMEMBER that I was recruited because the German government had donated Madiba a left-hand long-wheel-base Mercedes Benz, armour-plated vehicle and nobody could drive it. I was a mechanic by trade and I had come out of the movement and then they asked me to come and drive the car.

I REMEMBER that when we arrived at his residence, Genadendal, the convoy stops, he gets out, he thanks you, always by name, and talks to Shirley who would be at the door to welcome him. We used to wait until he went in, and the doors are closed then we depart. It was taking a while for Madiba to go into the house and to my surprise he turned around and came back to me. And then he remarked, 'Fuad is it because you don't want me to visit your house that you didn't tell me that your wife had a baby.' In any VIP protection the protocol is that you don't make small talk with your VIP. There has to be that distance. So I was quite taken aback, and I didn't know how to respond. I stuttered and eventually he said, 'When I'm in Cape Town the next time, I'm coming to visit this baby'.

I REMEMBER that I thought for a man as busy as he was, with the whole world consulting him about certain things he would forget but lo and behold a few weeks later someone from work called me. I was on a rest day or on some leave and someone called to say, 'You'd better prepare yourself, we are coming through, the convoy is on its way to your house.' It was the Old Man with Josina and Zelda and, of course, the whole security team arriving at my house. It caused such a lot of excitement in our area and they had to close that section of the road. We invited all the neighbours, they were quite free to come and meet the Old Man. That was my son Nabeel. He must have been maybe three months old then. I have a picture of the Old Man sitting with him on his lap.

I REMEMBER that when Madiba went to people to ask for money for his projects he would say, 'I am coming to ask you for money, but I'm not on my knees, I'm standing on my feet.'

Tony Trew

I REMEMBER how the international call to release Nelson Mandela and all political prisoners for a free South Africa helped re-kindle the ideals of a jaded generation.

I REMEMBER when he came to London not long out of prison. How he greeted reception committee members he had not known before: 'So pleased to meet you at last.' How we planned the Wembley concert programme to the last minute to cap the cost of world-wide satellite feeds.

I REMEMBER that at first sight of the freed prisoner, Wembley stopped him speaking as it roared with thanks and love and hope for seven minutes; and, when he had spoken his allotted minutes, he removed his glasses in what we would learn signalled words from the heart, to speak of his hope that OR recovering in Sweden would soon resume leadership.

I REMEMBER that he always dressed to convey a message: how he chose a suit for President Mandela to respect institutions, the Madiba shirt to embrace the people, the ANC colours for rallies; how, on the way to a media briefing, he chided me for my appearance and taught me the proper way to knot a tie.

I REMEMBER the connection when President Nelson Mandela went among the people, how he breached the line of protectors to be with the men, women and children of communities. And he would say afterwards, 'My batteries have been recharged.' How he would ignore his advisers when they said there was too little time to mobilise people, and in minutes fill the streets.

I REMEMBER in the dust of Winterveld, where he turned the millionth new tap to bring clean water, the light of love was in their eyes. In the cobbled streets of old Bangkok, as a thousand cameras rustled like leaves in the wind, a woman from Japan said: 'You think he is your president, but he is really the president of the world.'

I REMEMBER, too, just weeks ago, when I told a supermarket cashier in Dakar that I was from South Africa, how she sighed, 'Ah! Nelson Mandela! I remember Nelson Mandela!'

Faizel Moosa

I REMEMBER that a day or two after his release from prison Madiba left for Johannesburg. I was approached through Gadija Vallie, who was then in my dad's office, and she set up a meeting between myself and the also recently released Norman Yengeni, who said we needed to put together a protection detail for the ANC leadership as they come back into the country, for the Western Cape in particular. We had to just come up with a unit, develop it with our own resources and our own efforts, to make sure that when Madiba came back to Cape Town there was security around him. We were the first group in the Western Cape to provide protection for Madiba which was a real honour.

I REMEMBER Norman would tell us that Madiba was arriving on a certain date, then we had to arrange everything ourselves, the vehicles, the accommodation, the lunches, everything. Once, after he had finished his day around midnight or one o'clock in the morning he was up at four o'clock in the morning wanting to take a walk. I don't know where this old man got all the energy from. So we had to walk with him in the morning, a brisk walk in the morning, from the Ritz Hotel down towards Green Point. All along the route he would tell us the stories of where the boat, the *Susan Kruger*, landed when they came from Robben Island. He would walk all the way there and then all the way back and all along he would talk and would tell you little stories.

I REMEMBER when we took Madiba to Khayelitsha for a rally in the stadium. There were probably a hundred thousand people there. There were so many people that we just couldn't move the car. He got out of the car and greeted a woman with a child. Children were his Achilles' Heel.

I REMEMBER that if you told Madiba to walk this way then he wanted to go and greet a child in the crowd. A hundred thousand people are not easy but that was him.

I REMEMBER that Madiba was one of the few leaders we have worked with who would have a conversation with us in the car. He knew me by name and he knew the driver by name. Most of the others don't talk to their security detail; don't have a relationship with them. But Madiba had that personal touch. He was a man of that stature and he still knew your name – that to me already was an indication of his character.

I REMEMBER that people wanted to see him out of love but obviously the situation could get out of control so easily. At the end of the day you couldn't give him advice. You could tell him, 'Don't go, don't get out of the car and go into the crowd.' He would just do the total opposite. He wouldn't say anything and we would not question him about it. He just did his little thing, came back and didn't talk about it.

Thoko Mavuso

I REMEMBER that our President Mandela taught us to embrace other people and to forgive. Now that we are integrated our enemies are now our friends. If it wasn't for Madiba I am sure we would not have reached that point. We would still have that anger and that hatred; when we see a white person we would think of them as the oppressor. Madiba taught us that we have to forgive; not necessarily to forget, but we have to move on with life. If we don't forgive we won't see any change in our lives.

I REMEMBER that Madiba was a very strict person. I had the opportunity to work with him in an office and even in his home environment because most of the time I was at his residence so I got to know him that way.

I REMEMBER that we expected that because he was the president he would have special cooks but he was just an ordinary person.

I REMEMBER that he was a fatherly figure to the people who worked for him. When we had problems it was easy to go to him and tell him your problems. He would feel for you as a father. I didn't take him as my leader – I took him as a father.

Jessie Duarte

I REMEMBER at the tail end of the elections Madiba was convinced that we would win. He was quite buoyant and started to make notes about who would lead his office.

I REMEMBER that he was obsessed with administrative things. He would sit on a Monday and say, 'This is what we are going to achieve this week.' So for him those two weeks before the counting were quite critical, but he also started thinking about who would go into government with him.

I REMEMBER that Uncle Walter was his first and most important person to consult and they talked through a number of hard issues. And in those first weeks, as he was consulting, he also wanted to make sure that the demography of the Cabinet was non-racial. He had lists of names on his little notepad from the Indian community, from the coloured community, white people and African people. And then he would say, 'We've got to get the best from every community to be in this first Cabinet.' It was very important to him.

I REMEMBER that thanking people was a very big thing for him. A couple of days before the final election results came out and in that week Madiba phoned all the heads of state who had assisted the ANC in the election campaign. What impressed me is that he also called people like Buthelezi and people like Matanzima to say, 'We must go forward, we must go forward together.'

I REMEMBER when we were preparing for the inauguration I was touched by his involvement in the international guest list. There were people who just had to be there. He said, 'I'm not having this without Castro.' He wanted to know who said they were not coming and then he'd pick up the phone: 'Oh my brother, I believe you can't make it but you know I would really like you to be here.' And people couldn't say 'No' and they did come. We had more than one hundred and sixty heads of state.

I REMEMBER that in the time that I worked for him from 1990 to 1994 it was every day for seven days a week. Even when he went on holiday I went with him. He was an obsessive planner. He had these little calendars and he would write in small letters what he wanted to do. So I got quite clever. I thought, 'I must be one step ahead of this man', so I used to photocopy it and then start planning. So that when I went to him I would say, 'On your calendar you said you wanted to do one, two, three, four. This is the proposal I am making, we can do it in the following five or six days.' And he would be so happy and say, 'Ah! You've understood my plan.'

I REMEMBER that moment alone the hour before he made the inauguration speech, just alone him by himself, in that room, when I thought, it finally hit home, that they've achieved it, they've come this far, they've got to this point, something that had eluded them for twenty-seven years, that took a hard fight, that many people had died for. I've never seen Madiba sitting that quiet, he always fidgeted a bit, but there was that moment.

Wally Rhoode

I REMEMBER the first time I met Madiba. It was December 1987 and we had just come out of solitary confinement in Pollsmoor Prison. Warder Sergeant Christo Brand said he could get us movies but we need to go and ask for the projector. 'Who must we ask?' He said, 'You must go and ask Madiba.' In my mind Madiba had this middle parting in his hair and I didn't recognise him when we met. I recognised Ahmed Kathrada and Walter Sisulu. I'm standing there and he greets us and I say, 'Where's Madiba?' and he says, 'Here I am', and I said, 'It can't be because the picture I have of you is this'. But he says, 'Yes, but I'm also getting old.'

I REMEMBER that Richard Attenborough had given Madiba a copy of *The Last Emperor* and he said, 'Let the boys upstairs watch the movie, then they will behave themselves.' Because we went on in prison with boycotts and hunger strikes. So he gave us this movie and we were the first people to watch it and he was the second, before it was released in South African cinemas.

I REMEMBER in the Western Cape, just before the first elections, the ANC didn't have money so we organised people's houses for Madiba to stay in. The idea was the occupants could invite their close family, and take photos and eat, but then they must leave the house so Madiba can have it to himself.

I REMEMBER one morning while they were preparing breakfast for him, we were brought tea in chipped cups and sandwiches, as if we were servants. So we looked at the stuff and we decided we were not going to take it. Madiba came out and asked what the problem was. We said, 'Tata, we can't drink out of these cups.' Then he called the owner and he said, 'If you can't give these guys better food then you mustn't give me food because they are there to protect me.' From that day onwards we had decent food.

I REMEMBER when we arrived in Cape Town and Madiba said, 'We are not going to the hotel, I have some friends to stay with. If they phone you tell them I didn't make the plane.' And then he would spend the whole weekend in Cape Town, not going to a rally, nothing and just spend the two days with that couple. For us that was also sometimes a relief, given the hectic schedules that we had. We loved that when he was naughty because we knew we were just going to chill there the whole day.

I REMEMBER when we were on our way to a meeting in Khayelitsha from the Ritz Hotel, in the middle of the highway the whole convoy suddenly stopped. I jumped out because I was the planning officer. Madiba calls me to the car and says, 'Where's Jeremy?' I said, 'Why, Tata?' 'No, Jeremy must give me my change.' Then I called Jeremy and he went and Madiba said, 'Jeremy, next time when you buy me a newspaper put the change also with the newspaper.'

I REMEMBER when we were at an ANC fundraiser at the Lord Charles Hotel in Somerset West. To be a Number One bodyguard is sometimes a bad thing because when Madiba went to go and speak, I had to stand behind him. He was enjoying the attention and he was speaking and speaking. Trevor Manuel was sitting right at the back and was signalling for Madiba to stop. So I kicked Madiba to get his attention and he goes on talking and I kicked him again. He turned round and says, 'Wally, what's wrong?' I said, 'Tata, time.' He said, 'No, the food can get cold, they can warm it up again.' When we went out he said, 'You must never do that again, you know about my knees.' I said, 'But I tried to touch you and you just shrugged me off. I had to get your attention.' He says, 'Oh you guys think you know everything about me, nê?'

I REMEMBER the day before the elections, myself, Allan Boesak and Madiba flew from Cape Town to Lanseria in Sol Kerzner's plane. The menu of the day was crayfish and Madiba took out his fork and knife to eat it. I was looking at him and I thought, 'Must I tell him that he can't eat the crayfish with a knife and fork?' I went to Boesak and said, 'Please explain to this Old Man that he must crack the crayfish with his hands.' So Boesak tried. Madiba said, 'No, I don't eat goggas!' So Boesak asked him, 'So, why did you try with you knife and fork?' He said, 'No, I am trying to see what is inside this gogga.'

I REMEMBER that on the same flight there was turbulence. The one moment Madiba was talking and making jokes, the next moment he was silent and he was very still. I said to Jomo who was sitting next to the pilot, 'What's wrong with the Old Man?' He said, 'Wally, this is the second time we see this thing. The Old Man is scared of flying. Whenever there is turbulence he sits quietly and starts praying.' When we landed and we took him to his car, he called me aside and he said, 'Wally, next time you fly with me please don't smoke because you stink.'

I REMEMBER the week before Madiba became president we were preparing for the first opening of Parliament. Jeremy was a sniper and I was doing planning but we didn't have money. So I went to Barbara Masekela and then Jessie Duarte and they said I must speak directly to Tata. I deliberately spoke into his ear. I told him we needed R15 000 and he called Thomas Nkobi, 'Can you give them R50 000.00?' That was the first time the Department of Intelligence and Security of the ANC opened a bank account and we could pay people daily stipends.

I REMEMBER that when Madiba was president he had a meeting with a rebel leader from an African country. After three attempts to get him to South Africa, Madiba sent two of us in his own plane to fetch him. We hadn't searched him properly and had just looked in his briefcase. When I went to tell Madiba he had arrived, he asked us to send him through the metal detector. I said, 'But we don't do that to heads of state.' Madiba said, 'He's not a head of state, he's a rebel.' So we took him through the scanner and every time it would go off. I asked the late Tall Mtwazi to search him in the bathroom and he found a gun hidden on his body. Madiba said, 'Did you get anything on him?' I lied and said, 'No.'

Madiba said, 'No, I know you did because someone came to tell me you found a gun on him.'

I REMEMBER Madiba was chased away from Pretoria University by right-wing students and was insisting on going to Stellenbosch University. When we arrived these AWB students were threatening to chase him away. Madiba called Jeremy and said, 'Jeremy, I'm not leaving here today. You guys must do something.' Jeremy gave the students 'two seconds' to disperse but they refused. So Madiba asked us, 'What are you guys going to do?' We said, 'No, you are going to speak' and when Madiba went to the podium chaos broke out and for the first time in my whole life I drew my gun. Fortunately for us, Jeremy had recruited some of the Nusas Afrikaner students. There was a guy called Tiny, a very big Afrikaner guy. Bodyguards are supposed to get their principles out of the way but were fighting back. Madiba kept saying afterwards how proud he was of us.

Shiraz Moosa

I REMEMBER that whenever we took him into a crowd we always had to be on the look-out for children and babies because the minute he saw a child or a baby, all protocol was out of the window. The minute we saw a child we had our own plan how to deal with that. He would go into the crowd, straight to them. We had to protect him from the love of the people, not from people wanting to hurt him. But they probably could have hurt him because they loved him so much.

I REMEMBER that we would also have to be ready for him from four o'clock in the mornings in case he wanted to start his morning walks earlier than 5 am. Sometimes we would get there at four and we would wait for him but he had already slipped out of the house and was walking on his own in the estate. So it was almost like a cat and mouse game with him.

I REMEMBER that he would usually walk around the gardens in the estate and then one morning he said, 'Guys, today we are going to walk out onto the main road.' Now for that, it takes months and weeks of planning. No, he said that we were going to do it right now. So we had to call the local police to get assistance from them on Rondebosch Main Road.

I REMEMBER that we walked for an hour. It was getting light but it was nerve-wracking because you don't know what to expect. I don't think any previous president felt so safe walking in the public unannounced. Him walking on the outside without planning created a risk for us — that people would recognise him, and start phoning other people and a crowd would develop.

I REMEMBER the feeling that I had when I used to work with him in Parliament. I can't explain the feeling — it was almost spiritual. I still get emotional when I talk about it. I could feel it. Madiba had a calming presence, he didn't have to speak; he didn't have to say a word. It was just his presence when he walked into a room. Whatever thoughts you came with; it didn't matter. When you left that room it was with peace and harmony in your heart.

I REMEMBER that he had a lot of dignitaries come to see him at Tuynhuys and everybody, no matter how important they may have thought they were in the world, when they got to his office, there was a complete humbleness and calmness. He always wanted to make peace no matter what the circumstances.

Ashwyn Govind

I REMEMBER the day I placed a poster of Madiba at the foot of my bed and told myself one day I will walk with you.

I REMEMBER the day my first child was born while I walked the hills of Qunu with Madiba. When he received the news I remember him saying, 'Ashwyn you are now ready for responsibility.' I thought to myself, 'But Tata, I'm here protecting you from harm and you speak of me being ready for responsibility.'

I REMEMBER replaying these words in my mind on the day Madiba passed. Now I remember what Madiba was actually saying to me: 'Cherish the time you spend with your children as they are the future.' This I remember as part of Madiba's life which was very deep and close to his heart.

Willie Hofmeyr

I REMEMBER a briefing by the ANC Western Cape about what messages Madiba would be delivering the following day. It was late and he was at his hotel in his pyjamas and dressing gown. After listening patiently to the bickering for some time, he finally said: 'I want you to make sure the children are passed up to the front so they don't get crushed.'

I REMEMBER when Madiba visited District Six and spoke to people who had been forcibly removed thirty or forty years before. One woman told him that she had been so traumatised that in all that time she had never ventured out of the house they had moved her into.

I REMEMBER when Madiba would break away and launch himself into crowds of people to greet them, much to the frustration of his minders, who would have to run after him.

I REMEMBER how Madiba insisted on going for a walk at 5 in the morning because that was the time he woke up in prison.

I REMEMBER a blind white child reaching up to explore Madiba's face, while he remained perfectly still.

I REMEMBER when Madiba joined a meeting or lecture in progress, even though he never drew attention to himself, somehow everybody would know, turn around and rise to their feet. The meeting could only be called to order once he had sat down.

I REMEMBER when Madiba voted in his Rondebosch ward in the 1996 local election. When he arrived, he shook hands with everybody in the voting hall, then decided he wanted to greet everyone in the queue, at which point Cheryl Carolus led him firmly away.

I REMEMBER being moved to tears the only time I heard Madiba speak about the brutal hardships of the early years on Robben Island, with a slight tremor in his voice, but without a hint of bitterness.

Arch Sydow

I REMEMBER my first experience meeting Madiba. There was this tall figure, we are about the same height, the two of us, and our eyes met. I was thinking this is the man everyone was falling over their feet wanting to see. He radiated freedom and he had this enormous smile on his face. I think he was just very happy.

I REMEMBER that very early in the morning he asked me, 'Son, how are you?' And I said, 'No, I'm good, Tata. You look like you are excited. Where are you going?' We were about to enter the lift and he said he was going for a walk. He had this robust walk. I said, 'Hold on, hold on. You cannot just go and walk. I've got to look after you.' So we collected everybody and I had to quickly say, 'Look, this is the scenario. Madiba wants to go for a walk and he wants to walk to the harbour.' And the guys agreed, 'Let's go because he feels like going.'

I REMEMBER that Madiba never liked weapons. He never liked the sight of them, he never liked seeing them. I had to throw a jacket over my arm to hide my weapon.

I REMEMBER that he sent panic through our group at times because he used to greet everybody in the street. I think he was just reacting to his feeling of freedom. He was very excited so he would greet all the workers in the hotel. He couldn't care two hoots about what people thought about this, he was just this freedom-loving person with a smile on his face. He made you feel good.

I REMEMBER that after his walk he would come back to the hotel and get on an exercise bike for 15 to 20 minutes before he got ready for breakfast.

I REMEMBER that he was an ordinary man, a man who could rejoice and laugh. He had a gentleness and a beauty. He was not abusive. I could embrace him as a true comrade.

I REMEMBER seeing him in his room one day. He looked like a man who had a hard life. I saw sadness, endurance and yearning.

Russel Christopher

I REMEMBER when Madiba visited Sweden and we were staying in King Gustav's Castle. While going up for dinner, Madiba had hit his elbow against the bannister when he missed a step on the carpeted staircase. He didn't bother anybody about it during dinner. Jason Tshabalala and I slept in two separate rooms that led into Madiba's suite. Early the next morning Madiba popped his head into my room and said, 'Russel, Russel are you awake?' I pretended that I was wide awake and Madiba said, 'I would just like your assistance with something.'

I REMEMBER that while his elbow was not badly hurt it was swollen and sore. Madiba asked me to help him brush his teeth by holding up his elbow. On the same morning and two or three mornings afterwards, I would help him tie his shoelaces, his tie and the buttons on his shirt. After tying each shoe Madiba thanked me. He also thanked me for tying his tie. I got a thank you from him for every button I fastened.

Omar Suleman

I REMEMBER before 1994 we went to an ANC rally 'Madiba for the Cape' at the Allenby Stadium in the Retreat area. I was driving the support vehicle, which was a microbus. If anything should have happened – an attack or anything – the support vehicle would have the necessary logistical support. We entered the stadium and from where Madiba was sitting on the stage and from where I was entering, it was a very straight line. I navigated my way to get close to the podium, to get as close as possible to the stage.

I REMEMBER that in the evening when we went back to the Ritz Hotel Madiba insisted that I had endangered the lives of his supporters because I almost knocked over two people. I disagreed with this completely. Gary Kruser came to me and said we needed to go upstairs because Madiba was upset about this incident. And I said to Gary it couldn't have been because nobody was near my van, nobody, I was the driver of that van, but from where Madiba was sitting, he saw people going across and I suppose he saw the van moving and he saw people going across so in his mind he assumed that this van is going to knock over people. The command structure explained to Madiba that this was not the case and they had spoken to me about it and so on. We went upstairs because I needed to go and explain myself but for some reason something happened and to this day I wasn't reprimanded. I didn't get to see him which I was quite happy about because you will not answer back, you will leave it and just say sorry.

I REMEMBER when Madiba was at a venue in Wynberg. I wasn't part of the protection detail at that stage but I was sitting in the office with Hein Bezuidenhout and he asked me, if I was not busy with anything, to get a bulletproof car as they needed to get Madiba out in a decoy fashion. He was not going to come out with his regular convoy. I collected the Dolphin, one of the old bulletproof vehicles, and headed for the venue behind Wynberg Park. In about fifteen minutes Madiba entered the vehicle and, as usual, said, 'Good morning. How are you?' As we were driving towards the main road Hein was next to me in a much smaller convoy. Madiba says from the back seat, 'Excuse me I need to stop at a chemist.' I muttered to Hein: 'A chemist? That's a logistical nightmare.' Hein asked him, 'What is it that you need, Mr President?' And he says he needs blades and Prep cream. I thought to myself, 'There are a thousand people that can get this for you.' But he wanted to go.

I REMEMBER that we went to Noyes Photo Chemist in Kenilworth and we had to delay, delay, delay in order to get a proper logistical presence in that particular area. There was a whole array of things that we needed in order for the president to exit the vehicle in public. So within fifteen minutes everything was sort of in place. He exited the vehicle and walked with his security detail towards the chemist and somebody saw him and shouted,

'There goes Mandela!' Within the space of five minutes that place came to a standstill. It was chaos. Of course the buses stopped, the cars stopped. People were hooting. People were shouting and jumping and going completely crazy. They went into the chemist. I wasn't inside the chemist. I just had to keep the vehicle going. And what was supposed to be just a five-minute stop ended up to be almost thirty-five to forty minutes. Because Madiba wanted to meet the people and shake hands and it was absolutely crazy. Eventually, everything was done and he got into the vehicle. I said, 'Tata, the nation loves you.' And he said, 'Hmm.'

Xoliswa Ndoyiya

I REMEMBER when Madiba interviewed me for the job of his personal chef he only wanted to know from me if I could cook 'our food', the food he grew up with.

I REMEMBER if I didn't give him this traditional food for a few days he would say to me, 'What's wrong? Why are you not feeding me well?'

I REMEMBER how much Madiba liked pepper with his food. When he asked for 'a bit of pepper', what he really meant was 'a lot of pepper'. He liked a very generous shake of the pepper pot to make his throat glow.

I REMEMBER Madiba always treated me with kindness and respect.

I REMEMBER that Tata always reminded me, 'Xoli, as long as you are alive never give up and never forget your values and principles. Always remember who you are and where you are from.' I carry those words with me wherever I go.

Sam Shitlabane

I REMEMBER we were in Senegal, before we came to government, fundraising for the ANC with the late ANC Treasurer General Thomas Nkobi. Madiba met with the president of Senegal and I think it didn't go well. He was very upset and as we were going up to his suite he said, 'I think first thing in the morning we are leaving,' telling us and everybody. Then we got a call that the president was coming and they met again. So they then contributed. He was happy. As we were going up and Madiba said, 'Mr Nkobi, tomorrow morning you must fly to London and deposit the money.' From time to time he would call us and say, 'Chaps, how is the baby?' He wouldn't say 'money'.

I REMEMBER he once called me over as his protection team leader and asked me to go to Sacred Heart College where one of his grandsons was schooling. 'Go there and search the school because he lost his running shoes.' You can't just go to a school and search but I didn't want to argue with him so I went and spoke to the principal. He said they had internal processes and would follow up. So I went back to Madiba and I said, 'No Tata, it was not possible to search but the principal will report back.' He was happy and said, 'No man, you've done a very good job. I didn't know you needed a search warrant to search the school.'

I REMEMBER in 1994 we were preparing to go to a bosberaad in North West. I discovered that his personal assistant, the late Mary Mxadana, had not brought some documents. So I was talking to her and she was cracking jokes. I said, 'No Sis' Mary, we are late, where are the documents?' As I got into the car, I looked at Madiba in the rear-view mirror. He looked very angry. He started poking the back of my chair. 'Sam, no man, I don't like the way you are addressing Mary. That is not the way that you address a lady!' So I said, 'No Tata, we are working and she left the documents.' 'No man, don't answer! I hate this thing of yours when every time I say something, you have something to say.' So I kept quiet and it was kind of tense in the car. He says to Siphiwe, who was driving, 'Can you put the aircon on?' He was shifting the focus from me to the driver. So Siphiwe said, 'Tata, I am sorry the aircon is not working.' 'No man, you cannot tell the president that the aircon is not working. What kind of a security are you? It shows that you don't understand what you are doing.' On arrival he called me and tried to soften me. 'Sam you know sometimes you are told that this is how you have to treat a lady.' I said, 'Ah no, Tata, it's fine.'

I REMEMBER we were in Morocco for a holiday and he was with Aunt Graça. I was the team leader so he called me and said, 'Man, I want you to go and buy me Moët & Chandon champagne.' I didn't even know this Moët & Chandon and he had to spell it. He then gave me ten thousand US dollars. I thought this champagne must be very expensive. I think I must have used a hundred and something. I came back and I said, 'Tata, this thing is not expensive. Here's nine thousand and something US dollars.' He said, 'Wow. I didn't know. Gee whizz'.

Sathie Pillay

I REMEMBER driving Madiba to his Durban residence of King's House in 1994 and we received news that a group of old people and kids were at the main gate and they wanted to wave and greet Madiba. Since I was driving the main vehicle I was instructed that as we reach the gate I must accelerate so that Madiba won't see the people. I did just that. Madiba did notice the people and asked me why I was driving so fast up the driveway. I did damage control and said that the back-up car was close behind and I wouldn't be able to stop immediately if I braked fast. He then replied that I must ensure all those people standing by the gate must be brought up to the main house as he wanted to see them. We drove a Kombi to the gate and loaded in all the old ladies and kids and brought them to the house. He sat talking to the old ladies and played with the little kids who were running up and down in the lounge and onto him. The kitchen staff had to ensure that tea and biscuits were provided and Madiba spent a few hours entertaining the kids.

I REMEMBER that we took Madiba to Richmond Stadium for an ANC rally in 1995. There had been numerous political killings in the area. After the rally he wanted to go to Magoda, a local township headed by Sifiso

Nkabinde, who was a suspect in the killings. While I was driving Madiba in the Land Rover I explained to him that it was dangerous for us to take him there. He told me, 'There's no place in South Africa that is a No-Go area and any citizen must be able to travel freely in the country.' He insisted that we take him there.

I REMEMBER that while we were driving along the sandy road we saw Nkabinde and two bodyguards standing on the side of the road. Madiba said, 'Stop!' I made sure I passed the danger point and saw the South African Police Service Task Force disarming Nkabinde's bodyguards before we got out of the vehicle. Madiba walked up and down the road chatting and laughing with the old people and kids. He seemed so relaxed with no worries about the dangers that were lurking in that township. On his return to the car, he said, 'Sathie, you see there's no place in South Africa one must feel restricted to walk and express themselves.' I just nodded and said, 'Point taken, Tata.'

SR Moodley

I REMEMBER in 1999 when we were on his last campaign as the president in Mthatha in a suburb called Ngangelizwe. It was my turn that week to be the Number One bodyguard, which is the person walking immediately behind him. We had to walk about eight hundred metres through the street and of course there were a lot of people on the side and a lot of people joining the walk. At one stage he turned to me and he asked, 'Is the PAC also here?' So I looked at the person he was pointing towards and he was wearing a T-shirt that said '2 P-A-C'. It was Tupac Shakur, the rapper. I think Madiba only saw the P-A-C. So I had to whisper to him to say, 'No, it's the rapper who was shot recently' and he said, 'Oh! Okay'. It had been quite prominent in the news so he might have picked it up.

I REMEMBER when my wife and daughter, Sameera, came to visit me while I was working in Parliament. I was in Government Avenue, just chatting with them quickly, and Madiba happened to come out to the gate in Government Avenue outside Tuynhuys, directly opposite the rear door. Since I was there I took up a position. He simply loved children and my wife and daughter went closer to see him and he automatically put his hand out towards my daughter and offered a greeting and she, being two-and-a-half, pulled back and then he said, 'I've never been so insulted in my whole life.' I still needle her about it.

I REMEMBER his general message everywhere was love for people and his number one message to the youth was education, education, education. Every opportunity he got, he emphasised that.

I REMEMBER I was with him in the tornado in 1998 on 15 December. It was quite a day for us because the world's press then basically descended on the small town of Mthatha. Of course it was a big occasion for us. We were blessed to come through this tragedy because twenty-six people died and something like a hundred and fifty were injured. We actually saw people being struck by hail and falling right in front of us. Two of our guys on the inside thought it was an explosion because the glass door had blown down and crashed with quite a force. And the roof lifted; we on the outside could see those big roof sheetings whirling in the air and the electricity pylons falling one after the other, blocking the road and massive trees were uprooted. We had to take him to safety. He was very calm through everything and when we got back to the house he told our team leader then, Superintendent Mtwazi, that we have done very very well and that he is not going anywhere and we must take the afternoon off. He offered some money for us to go and buy some food, about R800. We were very adamant to our commander that, no, we are doing our duty and we refused to take the money for it. He was obviously now in a bit of a tizz because he couldn't take the money back to Madiba. We sorted it out later, I think, we had a party when he left eventually.

I REMEMBER towards the end of his presidency he would often visit book shops, often spending an hour and buying nothing but looking around. He loved books. And obviously there would be a crowd when he came out and I almost got the sense that he fed off the souls of people, he got energised from interacting with people. He would spend half an hour, forty-five minutes, an hour in a bookshop and then spend another hour chatting to the people outside. Some of the people, after shaking his hand, would just break down crying. That was the impact that he had.

I REMEMBER, although I started working with him in 1993, the very first time I met him and shook his hand was in 1995. I immediately felt an aura come across from him, a powerful aura and when we were doing campaigns and things like that, he was the only person I have come across who could get such a reaction from the crowd, that we would feel that vibration in our chests. I was blessed and honoured; it was an absolute privilege having those few years working with him.

I REMEMBER his phenomenal memory. At the Michael Jackson concert, again I was the Number One bodyguard and he was in one of those suites and there was a white gentleman in front and he called me and said, 'Call that gentleman in,' which I did and then he said to this guy, 'I know we've met before but I can't quite place it,' and the gentleman said, 'Yes, Mr Mandela we met last year in Paarl when somebody introduced me to you.' Just an introduction but the face stuck. Over a year later, thousands of people later, but he picked up that face in the crowd. He just greeted him and then the man left.

I REMEMBER his ability to win people over. We were in Stellenbosch in 1996 or thereabouts and I was there before his arrival and obviously Stellenbosch was very conservative and I could hear the murmurings and the chats among the people there. A lot of them were white farmers and it was sort of negative towards this whole visit but, after he finished, they were completely won over. They were clapping the loudest, the hardest and were wanting an audience with him, you know, to say, 'How can we get in and build this new South Africa.'

Hein Bezuidenhout

I REMEMBER when we were in New York City in 2000. It was extremely cold and snowing. There was a fundraiser at the Waldorf Astoria attended by many prominent businessmen, politicians and celebrities, such as Evander Holyfield and Henry Kissinger, to name a few. As protectors, we were only interested in the movie stars and requested Zelda to convince Madiba to broker a meeting for us. At the end of the function the distinguished guests lined up for photo opportunities with Madiba. When it got to the movie stars Madiba in his dry humoristic way instructed them to pay. They were clearly taken aback. 'What do you mean?' 'You need to take a photo with my security.' They obliged and Zelda whisked them into an adjacent suite where we were waiting patiently. Prof Gerwel, Zelda and my colleagues (Cassie and Marnitz) were over the moon to meet and pose for photographs with Robert de Niro and Whoopi Goldberg. We had a rookie US Secret Service detail with us and their team leader, an avid de Niro fan, went ballistic when he noticed Mr de Niro. We fortunately managed to 'protect' Mr de Niro from this annoying fan who was banging on the suite door. The honour was repeated the next morning when I had to host Mr de Niro and his family for a few minutes while Madiba was getting ready to see them.

I REMEMBER on one of Madiba's early morning walks in Cape Town a vehicle stopped next to us at about 5:30 am in Newlands Avenue. It was the bread deliveryman doing his rounds. He introduced himself and invited Madiba to his wedding. Weeks later Madiba was in Cape Town and on a Saturday morning he informed us that he wanted to attend 'This chap's' wedding. We were handed an address of where the ceremony was intended. My colleague, Captain David van Aswegen, and I rushed to the site discovering that the ceremony was finished and that the entourage was off to Rondebosch for wedding photographs. We then rushed to a public park located in Main Street in the Newlands/Rondebosch area popular among Muslim couples. On arrival there were hundreds of couples in bright outfits all mingling and taking pictures. In the meantime Madiba grew impatient and was en route in his motorcade to us. The only problem was that although we had the couple's names we had no clue what they looked like. As Madiba's motorcade rolled in to park Assie and I managed to find the couple. Needless to say many other couples got the surprise of their lives and also had photos taken with Madiba. All of this made our security job extremely hard. However, we came out tops with a lot of, as we called it, 'Madiba's Luck'.

I REMEMBER when Jill Daniels, the youngest member of our unit, was turning twenty-one and Madiba wanted to buy her something for her birthday. 'Do we still have some of those books of mine in stock?' he asked, referring to *Long Walk to Freedom*. I said we did not so he asked how much they cost as he wanted us to take him to the bookshop to buy a copy. Knowing what chaos such a trip to the Gardens Centre, Cape Town would cause, I stalled and went on a frantic search for a crisp copy of *Long Walk to Freedom*. Sergeant Symington, a policeman at Tuynhuys, just happened to have a new copy that he wanted Madiba to sign. It still had the price sticker on – R250. I rushed back to the president to announce my find. Madiba was very perturbed when I informed him of the price. 'What? I told them that this book should never cost more than R150!' He was now even more determined to visit the book shop. I kept saying we could not go and he kept insisting. So I walked out of the president's office and confiscated Symington's cherished book. At least Madiba then let go of his plans to visit the shops. He scribed a message for Jill in the book and reluctantly handed me R250 to pay for a copy of his own biography.

I REMEMBER when Madiba got the Freedom of Swellendam. Llewellyn Weideman, protector driver, and I were in the car with the local mayor – a reverend. We were waiting at the Swellendam Airfield on Madiba's arrival. The mayor went quieter and quieter as Madiba's arrival grew closer. He seemed terrified at the idea of meeting Madiba. When Madiba got into the back seat of the borrowed navy-blue Land Rover Discovery – we had to borrow cars in those days – there was a full ten to twelve seconds of dead silence. It felt like an eternity. Madiba just sat politely next to the mayor. I politely turned in my seat and looked at the mayor and said, 'You can talk to the president now' and he started introducing himself. After that he never stopped.

I REMEMBER in 1999 we took Madiba and Mrs Machel on a vacation hideaway in the quaint fisherman's village of Paternoster in the Western Cape Province. Madiba and Mrs Machel stayed at Wayne and Sandy's Oystercatcher Guest House. We maintained a low profile and took them in unmarked cars to see the flamingos and the flowers. We were only discovered after two days when Madiba decided to have lunch at the Voorstrand Restaurant located right on the main beach. Madiba casually strolled into the restaurant and took up the table with the best sea view, pre-booked for him under a different name. The news spread like wildfire and within minutes the whole village was down on the beach. There was a whale splashing about in the shallow waters right in front of us. As there were many children gathered on the beach they were blocking Madiba's view. Madiba got a bit agitated and asked me to request the children to move so that he could enjoy the unique whale moment. Zelda jumped into action and bought sweets at the local store. Within seconds she managed to coax the children away, allowing Madiba to appreciate the view. On exit the whole town formed a guard of honour for Madiba and Mrs Machel. Madiba shook everyone's hand, including the dirty sweaty hands of the construction workers who were working across the street.

Sam Nwamusi

I REMEMBER when Madiba became president he first stayed in the Presidential Guest House because Marike de Klerk really liked the presidential residence and wanted to stay there with former president FW de Klerk. Madiba preferred to leave her there. Me, and the late Victor and Gigi stayed there with Madiba.

I REMEMBER one morning he handed me the car keys knowing that it was not my job to drive him and insisted that I must take him 'home'. I made a mistake because now that he was the president he was not allowed to be driven anywhere alone. He was so demanding that I felt obliged to drive him, for the first time. I thought he wanted to go to his house in Houghton but found out when we got there that he wanted to go to Soweto to see the family of a friend of his from the Pan Africanist Congress who had passed away. The other group of protectors meanwhile went to the Presidential Guest House in Pretoria to find that Madiba was not there. My commander was very angry with me. He shouted at me and even at Madiba.

I REMEMBER the only other time he persuaded me to drive him was early one morning about 3 o'clock, we were at his home in 13th Avenue Houghton and Madiba had been told that Joe Slovo had passed away. He came to me and said, 'Let's go to Joe Slovo's house.' The 'Static' uniformed police who guarded Madiba's house opened the front passenger door of the Volkswagen Jetta for him and I found myself persuaded by him to drive him to Joe Slovo's house. I had another serious problem with my commander, he even wanted to expel me from the convoy. From that day I was suspended from being a close protector and was made Commander of Madiba's Static police guard because I had been 'ill-disciplined'.

I REMEMBER one day Madiba came out and asked me to take him to the ANC headquarters at Shell House in downtown Johannesburg. I couldn't drive him because of my record of taking him places without authorisation. I told him I didn't have the car keys. Madiba walked out of the gate down to the main road, Central Street. There was a lady standing on the side of the road and she hailed a taxi. We all got into the taxi. Madiba didn't even have one cent in his pocket so I paid. The lady recognised Madiba and started screaming, 'Tata!' Madiba responded immediately, 'Hi. How are you?' Everybody in the taxi greeted Madiba.

I REMEMBER that before we reached Shell House, the taxi driver dropped the other passengers in Hillbrow. I was scared because we thought the taxis belonged to Inkatha members and there was animosity with the ANC. When we got to Shell House the driver wanted to refund Madiba but he said, 'Keep it, keep it.' But it was my money, not his. He never refunded me.

I REMEMBER one day Madiba told me he wanted to go to his old house in Orlando. We went in advance to check the route to the house in Orlando West. We picked up Madiba and went in the convoy but he diverted us to Orlando East. I never knew that Madiba had a house in Orlando East but I then found out that he had lived there in 1946. He directed me to the house and didn't get lost.

I REMEMBER when Madiba insisted on going to the 2009 ANC's 'Siyanqoba' election rally at Ellis Park. We said, 'Tata you are tired, you have to rest.' He refused. Mrs Machel tried to convince him but Madiba is Madiba. We went to that rally.

I REMEMBER how Mrs Machel taught Madiba about protocol. He used to violate protocol and stop the car while the convoy was moving, not respecting security and protocol. If he saw something and wanted to stop the car he just touched Bra Mike and he applied the brakes. Sometimes the cars in the convoy nearly bumped into each other because of Madiba.

I REMEMBER the excitement of the crowd when Madiba appeared at the closing ceremony of the 2010 FIFA World Cup Final in Johannesburg. It was the first time it was hosted in Africa. I walked in front of the golf cart driven by my colleague, Motsamai and carrying Madiba and Mrs Machel. We went right around the stadium as the people were cheering. Then we took him home.

Zanele Riba

I REMEMBER being in the lift at our offices in Shell House, the headquarters of the ANC. The doors opened on the ground floor and there stood Madiba and his security. I was shell-shocked, I had not expected anyone in the lift as I took it on the ground floor and I did not know that it could go down to the basement. He just said, 'Good morning.' I did not know how I should respond.

I REMEMBER when Thoko called me to go upstairs to Madiba's office with her. The big book about Muhammad Ali was on his desk and Thoko and I started to page through the book, and as we were doing so, Madiba looked at us and said, 'Are you two young ladies also boxers?'

I REMEMBER when my daughter missed out on having her photograph taken with Madiba and the children of his other staff members. One day they made an appointment with Thobeka and another child. She was about four or five years old and very shy. And short. When she was standing with Madiba he asked her name. She replied, 'Thobeka' and he being so tall and far away from this little girl said, 'Oh Thembeka'. She was too shy to correct him.

Barbara Masekela

I REMEMBER when I started working for him, one of the things he told me was 'You can say anything to me, and I'll never be angry with you' and that was true, up until I left.

I REMEMBER that from the very beginning he treated me like a comrade and a friend that he could confide in as he did with everybody else who was working in his office. The remarkable thing about his office was that it was almost entirely women and it worked very well because we were focusing on the larger picture of him being able to fulfil his mission, none of us were hoping to become this or the other through him.

I REMEMBER that Madiba was the only person who had the courage to engage with anybody and find out what they were thinking. One of the beautiful things about him is that he thought with his heart.

I REMEMBER that Madiba was a very good student and he had the gift of internalising what he was told and making it his own. Madiba insisted on knowing and understanding his briefings and he would have his little notebook at home and study. So when he spoke about the subject it came out perfectly.

I REMEMBER that he was also critical. Even with his speeches he would change subtleties and say, 'I want this like this and this word.' If you gave him a draft speech he would read it, he wouldn't make long annotations, but the ones he made were such that by the time he made the speech it was his own.

I REMEMBER most sharply about him his inclusiveness. I don't mean in the big picture thing of politics, the races and all that, but to everybody around him. Even in his office, nobody was too important.

I REMEMBER that he had a routine, but he also had silly things like he didn't want us to work after hours. He didn't want us to come into the office before hours. He just had no clue about how much work was involved, that it was not a nine-to-five thing. You had to work all the time to keep up.

I REMEMBER his enthusiasm and almost child-like wonder in the experience of introductions. Irrespective of the status of the individual, every new encounter was like a rediscovery of the novelty and complexity of human nature. His face lit up and he was able to forget himself for an innocent moment as he reached out his hand to touch another human being.

Moosa Ramjoo

I REMEMBER sometime in 1993 in KwaZulu-Natal during Madiba's election campaign, he was staying in a hotel on Marine Parade in Durban, directly opposite the beach. I was part of his protection team. One day at about midday, we were informed that Madiba wanted to take a walk on the beach. We grouped in the foyer of the hotel and when he arrived from his room we proceeded to walk along Marine Parade. I was the 'lead man', a term for the protector who is leading the way. After several stops, while Madiba was chatting with street vendors, we went onto the beach. Madiba indicated that he wanted to go onto the pier.

I REMEMBER that when we were walking on the pier Madiba was excited to see surfers jumping off with their surfboards and wanted to know why they were doing that. I explained to him that it was tiring for the surfers to get past the waves from the shallow side and if they jumped off the pier they would avoid the breakers. He remarked, 'How clever.' Madiba stopped a teenager and greeted him and asked him if they taught surfing at school. The young man replied, 'No, Mr Mandela, you have to learn surfing like you learn to play soccer or golf.'

Goolam Aboobaker

I REMEMBER I was working in the Cabinet Secretariat of the Office of the President. In 1995 the activist Lisa Seftel came to inform Cabinet on specific labour legislation. As soon as she took her seat, Mr Mandela went up to her, shook her hand and inquired after the health of her father. Before she could start her presentation, Mr Mandela himself introduced her, emphasising that she was very active in the struggle and remarked that she was also the daughter of the well-known medical doctor Prof Harry Seftel. It impressed me that he took such a deep interest in the personal lives of those who mattered to him.

I REMEMBER how in 1990 I saw this in action on the political level. When I was employed at the University of the Western Cape in the Office of the Vice-Chancellor Prof Jakes Gerwel, we were expecting a visit from Mr Mandela. Our Rector, Prof Gerwel and Deputy Rector, Prof Jaap Durand had gone to the airport to meet him. However, Mr Mandela arrived at the University before they had and was not prepared to leave the vehicle before he was met by an official from the Rector's office. These being pre-mobile phone days, we were unable to contact either Gerwel or Durand. I was accordingly sent to receive him in my jeans and T-shirt! Having been caught unawares, I later ensured that a formal jacket and tie was kept in my office.

I REMEMBER that I took Mr Mandela to the Rector's office and asked him whether he would like some tea or coffee, whereupon he requested a glass of tap water or soda water at room temperature. After explaining to him that my responsibilities as 'Special Assistant' to Prof Gerwel included advising him on how the university could be transformed to become 'an intellectual home of the left' and to be an 'honest interlocutor', Mr Mandela went on to ask a range of questions: What was meant by creating an intellectual home of the left at the university? He had read about many student protests at the university and wanted to know how students related to this project. He appeared to be very keen to know more about the black universities and in particular about the University of Zululand. Fortunately, I did not have to answer his questions, because Prof Gerwel arrived back in his office!

Bob Nicholls

I REMEMBER when we left Ellis Park after South Africa had played against Zambia on the day of the inauguration, President Mandela saw a police officer on the side of the road and stopped the convoy to chat to him.

I REMEMBER at the pick-up point where he was about to board a helicopter to fly back to Pretoria, he had a phone in his hand and asked me to assist him to phone Deputy President Thabo Mbeki. Cellphones were quite new and he didn't know how to use it and neither did I. Luckily one of the pilots knew how to use a mobile phone and could show me how to call him.

I REMEMBER that night before he went to bed on his first night as president, Madiba insisted on thanking all the members of his security team. It blew my mind that after such a long day he still found time to shake each person by the hand and to thank them personally. He noticed that one member of his security team, the man who drove his car, was not there. He said, 'I would like to thank him too.' So we found him. I think he was asleep in the car as he had been up since 4 am. We woke him and brought him to the president.

Linga Moonsamy

I REMEMBER a young girl, of about seven or eight years old, from the neighbourhood where Madiba lived, came to his house and insisted on seeing him. We stopped her at the gate but he got wind of it and said, 'Allow her in, chaps.' She walked straight up to him, sitting in his favourite cane chair in the garden reading the newspaper. He put the newspaper down and she stood next to him and she looked at him and said, 'How old are you?' No greeting, no nothing. And he said, 'Well, I'm very old. I don't remember my age.' And you could see this strange look in her eyes. She then said, 'You were in jail?' He said, 'Yes I was in jail.' She said, 'For how long?' And he said, 'Well, I can't remember, it was a long time ago.' And she looked at him for a while and then she said, 'You know you are a very stupid old man. You don't know how old you are, and you don't know how long you were in jail. Can you count?' He just burst out laughing and gave her a huge hug and said, 'You are welcome anytime to see me.'

I REMEMBER that one day when he was going out of the house he saw the cigarette butts some of us had dropped. They were all over the paving where the cars were parked. Walter Mazola, one of the protectors, was with him and he asked him, 'Who threw these cigarettes butts?' Walter used to smoke but in all his wisdom he decided to say, 'No, it's Linga.' Madiba said to me, 'Chap, next time you throw your butts here, I will make you pick it up.' I apologised.

I REMEMBER when I was Number One, the person in the vehicle with him, I would normally calculate what time we had to leave and try to have a cigarette so that he doesn't get the smell. But on a few occasions he caught us off guard. He would come fifteen minutes earlier and the cigarette smell would still be on my clothing. Once when I got into the vehicle, Madiba asked Bra Mike, 'Mike can you smell stompies in this vehicle.' Mike said, 'Yes Tata, yes Tata.' I said, 'Sorry I was smoking.' And he said, 'When are you going to leave this smoking of yours?' And I said, 'Tomorrow, Tata.' And he said, 'Linga, you know I am like your grandfather and you should not lie to me. Yesterday you told me you would give up smoking tomorrow. Today you are telling me you will give up smoking tomorrow. And I suppose tomorrow you will tell me you are giving up smoking tomorrow.'

I REMEMBER Madiba used to love deciding suddenly to visit a shop. I don't know if he got a kick out of seeing us struggling with crowds. We would leave, for example, the Union Buildings on our way home and he'd say, 'Linga, you know we need to pass a bookshop.' I said, 'What do you need at a book shop?' 'No, I need to go and buy a book.' I said, 'No Tata, give me the money and I'll buy the book.' 'No, you see you wouldn't know what book I want.' I called some of our guys and sent them to the

CNA to inform the management that the president is on his way and they should shut the doors because we don't want chaos when we get there. The manager did not take them seriously and said 'No president will come here'. When the convoy arrived, once one person saw it was Madiba, everybody went crazy and the word spread like wildfire. It took us almost half an hour to find the book because he was greeting everyone and there's shouting and screaming. It was just a normal hardcover notebook. When we eventually got to the till, he pulls out his wallet, he looks at the lady and he takes out $100 note. And he says, 'Do you accept dollars?' She said, 'No we only take rands.' So I had to pay.

I REMEMBER whenever you try to push someone out of the way he would say, 'Ah, you know, chaps I understand you are doing your job, but when you push people you must have a smile on your face.'

I REMEMBER I was assigned first to Kathy Kathrada and then moved to Madiba, they used to call each other 'madala' — old man. So one day when Kathy was at the house he saw me and said, 'You know madala, this chap used to be my chap? And you took him away from me?' And Madiba says, 'Well, he's now my chap madala, get your own chap.'

I REMEMBER one day we were driving from the Union Buildings and as we got to Houghton he saw this lady, I must say she was quite huge. He said, 'You should go and approach that lady and take her to run with you chaps.' We said, 'Tata we don't know that lady.' He said, 'Go and introduce yourselves.'

I REMEMBER when it got closer to his term ending, we had two guys to work the nightshift with Madiba. One night the late Paul Chauke and I were on duty and Madiba called for me. I went up to him and he said, 'Linga, can you iron these trousers for me?' So I looked at him and I said, 'Tata. I can't iron.' 'Man, what is wrong with you?' 'I don't know how to iron.' He says, 'Go and learn and try.' I said, 'If I burn your pants I can't afford to replace them.' He said, 'Take my trousers and go and learn to iron.' I took them and went to Paul and said, 'The President says you must iron his trousers.'

Lolo Tabane

I REMEMBER when Her Majesty Queen Elizabeth II visited South Africa in 1995. Madiba and Her Majesty were going to use two different lifts. Madiba preceded the Queen, and we were to wait for her to enter her lift. The plan was that the lift operators would then simultaneously drive the two lifts. As Madiba was busy greeting the operator and talking to him he just hit the button and the lift went up. We lost the Queen. I turned to Madiba and said, 'Tata we have lost the Queen' and explained to him what had happened. He calmly turned to the operator and explained in Xhosa that we have lost the Queen and that we should go and fetch her. There was no reproach from him and no animosity.

I REMEMBER that when we visited Denmark in 1999 Madiba was supposed to wear the National Order bestowed to him by Queen Margrethe II when she visited South Africa in 1996. This did not happen due to unforeseen circumstances. I asked Mrs Machel to ask Madiba to apologise to the Queen on our behalf for the mistake and left them to finish their breakfast. When I came to fetch them for their engagement with the Queen, Madiba was wearing the National Order meant for night time but it was during the day. It was his humble way of apologising.

I remember that the Queen understood but the people of Denmark were asking us as his protocol people why we made him wear it during the day. We heard that many citizens felt offended by what they perceived to be our incompetence.

Jan van der Walt

I REMEMBER, during one of my first flights with Mr Mandela, we transferred from his plane to a military Oryx helicopter. All the delegates and bodyguards boarded the helicopter, then Mr Mandela. I was last to board and there were no more seats available. I could not stay behind and decided to sit on the floor of the helicopter. Mr Mandela had a reserved seat, which was big enough for two people. He gestured to me to join him. As a nineteen-year-old, this gesture meant the world to me.

I REMEMBER the day all the medical personnel had lunch with Mr Mandela at his official residence, Mahlamba Ndlopfu. It must have been the quietest lunch in history. I sat there thinking that just two short years before I had learnt about Mr Mandela in high school history, and here I was having lunch with someone who is prominent in world history. I remember Mr Mandela as a humble and selfless person who cared for all he met.

Priscilla Naidoo

I REMEMBER when President Mandela attended the United Nations General Assembly in New York City, he asked me to invite the South African media contingent to join him on his early morning walk in Central Park the following morning. I had informed the media that if they wanted to join the President they should be at the hotel before 5 am. It was a beautiful, cool autumn morning as President Mandela emerged from the lift. He was surprised to see that there were no media people at the hotel and decided to continue on his walk with his close protectors and myself. The American Secret Service agents were cruising nearby in black vehicles and others dressed in dark suits walking parallel to us. When we returned to the hotel, we saw disappointed-looking media standing in the foyer. President Mandela greeted all of them and asked them to join him on another walk. He thoroughly enjoyed a second walk in Central Park and the media representatives were overjoyed at his kind gesture.

I REMEMBER the exquisite red rose, beautiful smiles, laughter and love between President Nelson Mandela and Graça Machel as they were photographed for a special *Sunday Independent* exclusive Valentine's Day photo

– not an easy assignment as one can imagine (one doesn't make such demands to one's elders) but I managed to pull it off.

I REMEMBER 17 March 1997 when Princess Diana was on a private visit to her brother who lived in Cape Town. The media were chasing her two convoys – a real one and a decoy – but they could just not get the photo. They were so excited after I sent a late-night alert inviting the media for a photo opportunity with President Mandela and Princess Diana at Genadendal, the president's official residence in Cape Town. I had the great honour to receive Princess Diana and conduct her and the British High Commissioner to the lounge. While we waited for President Mandela to join Princess Diana, I briefed her on the photo opportunity. I told her that the journalists may ask her a question or two and she said she would be happy to respond. I remember her sitting on the sofa in her dark blue dress with white spots, her long legs crossed, right over left, and she gazed at the ceiling and asked questions about the house. She was so impressed by the design and architecture. I was amazed that a princess who lived in a palace was saying how impressed she was with the house.

I REMEMBER when President Mandela finally entered the lounge Princess Diana stood up and with a big smile walked towards him. They greeted each other warmly and he also shook hands with the High Commissioner and invited both of them to sit. They chatted for a while and when it was time for the photo opportunity, I invited them to the veranda where the media were waiting patiently.

A smiling President Mandela proclaimed loudly that it must be the princess the media had come to see because he never got so much media for his press engagements. It was such a beautiful and warm interaction with the media who all told me how grateful they were to have had the opportunity to have seen Princess Diana. Her radiant beauty and humility touched all those who were present.

I REMEMBER December 2013, as thousands of mourners paid their respects to our world icon I was standing in the Union Buildings garden getting a preview of a new statue of Nelson Mandela to be unveiled on 16 December.

I REMEMBER almost fainting when I saw the huge statue. President Mandela's outstretched arms embracing us all looked so life-like. Every day visitors, local and international, continue to embrace the father of the nation and the world whose message of unity and nation-building radiates towards the horizon and reminds us all to embrace humility, loyalty, compassion, faithfulness and love among each other.

Stephanus 'Fanie' Pretorius

I REMEMBER waiting for Madiba to arrive at the Union Buildings for his first day of work as President of South Africa. He gave me a message to give to the staff, namely that they would be welcome to remain working in the Office of the President provided that their performance was satisfactory. I asked him if he could tell them himself. When he entered the room where about eighty staff members sat waiting for him, there was absolute silence. After a few seconds, Madiba said: 'Well, I am a bit pressed for time, but I would like to shake hands with all of you.' He moved from left to right in the large circle, shaking the hand of every staff member. About halfway through, he reached a lady from the finance department who shook his hand with a rather solemn expression on her face. Maybe she just reflected, better than the rest of us, the tension that everybody experienced at that moment. The next moment everybody burst out laughing and the ice was broken when Madiba asked her in Afrikaans, 'Is jy kwaad vir my?' [Are you angry with me?]

I REMEMBER the evening of 9 September 1994 when about 500 former freedom fighters were gathered on the lawns of the Union Buildings demanding equal rights and pay in the new South African army. They agreed to leave if the president would speak to them. I met Madiba at his official residence but instead of travelling with his security staff (as I suggested) he got into my rented Toyota Corolla and said, 'Security is going to be upset about this.' I was proud of myself for actually finding the narrow dirt road that allowed me to drive onto the lower terrace of the Union Buildings, where a few hundred men were awaiting us, cheering loudly when they saw the president.

Trevor Manuel

I REMEMBER a rather curious incident when, about a year after he stepped down as president, he telephoned me a few times, seeking to arrange a meeting. My natural reaction was to commit to going to his home in Houghton to see him. He was very insistent that such an approach would not work, as it needed to take place in my office.

I REMEMBER that as the intrigue around this grew, I initiated an offline discussion between Patti, my PA, and Zelda, his PA. No interventions would work – it needed to be in the minister's office. Then followed discussions about the logistics and, since the meeting would take place around lunchtime, the Ministry would provide lunch, on the advice of Zelda. This was not the easiest task since the National Treasury was low on facilities, it had no catering and the bulk of refreshments were then still provided by civil service 'tea clubs'.

I REMEMBER Madiba arrived for the meeting on the appointed date in early July and, as can well be imagined, there was complete pandemonium right across the twenty-seven floors of the offices of the National Treasury, then at 240 Vermeulen Street, Pretoria. Thankfully, technology had not evolved to the point where mobile phones had cameras, and selfies belonged to the distant future. Notwithstanding that, all the staff formed an unbelievably long queue to shake his hand.

I REMEMBER with the preliminaries disposed of, the lunch meeting could start. On this issue too, Madiba was insistent that it be 'under four eyes'. It turned out to be a minor matter relating to the calculation of the pension of a former president. It could easily have been disposed of in a quick visit to his home, or, in fact, even telephonically.

I REMEMBER that the clarity that I sought was about his insistence on coming to the minister's office — I was many decades his junior and I related to him as a son, I purposely called him 'Tata', and sometimes he would retort with terms like 'Boy' or 'Son'. I popped the question and, 'Oh', he said, 'I promised my wife that I would always respect ministers and their office. We agreed that since I was no longer the president, I should not expect ministers to come to me.' This single story speaks volumes about Madiba's (sometimes too-literal) interpretation of servant leadership.

Simon Mothibi Mathatho

I REMEMBER being in a convoy with Madiba just after he left his house on the way to Shell House in the city. After driving one block a guy said on the radio, 'Stop stop. The principal says we must stop. He says there is a stompie in his car.'

I REMEMBER that Madiba was pointing his finger and insisting there was a cigarette butt in the car. It turned out to be the bodyguard Kitt who was a big smoker. When he got into the car Madiba smelled cigarettes. He was taken out of the car and replaced with someone else.

Donny Thebus

I REMEMBER sitting in the official vehicle with President Mandela in a Northern Cape town. It was, as usual, boiling hot and the old 'BMW left-hand-drive panzer' aircon was not helping to alleviate the heat. The president had a European dignitary with him in the vehicle. The dignitary remarked that it was unfortunate that 'your party', the African National Congress, did not receive a two-thirds majority in the national elections. The president's response was diplomatic and unapologetic, and he stated that at times, where a party such as his with overwhelming support, it is not good to hold such dominant state power and that this could aid his government's reconciliatory stance.

I REMEMBER on 15 December 1998, I was deployed as a close protector with President Mandela in the official vehicle on route to a pharmacy in downtown Mthatha. The president wanted to purchase a bar of soap, the same one he used in prison. I remember as we drove on the N2, the sky was dark with the presence of an imminent storm. We entered the pharmacy and while being assisted we moved close to the back of the pharmacy when suddenly without warning the shop window's glass 'exploded'. Instinctively we dived the president to the floor; Inspector Willie Siljeur dived below the president to prevent him from hitting the tiled floor. It was a surreal moment as we had to say to the president that we needed to get up (from the floor) and start moving. In that instant the team leader, the late Superintendent Thobile Mtwazi, advised the team that it was a storm. We moved the president to a small consultation room where a few people were hiding; we moved them out and brought in the president. I explained to him what had just happened and asked him if he was hurt. I assumed he would be angry but he responded in a statesmanlike manner: 'Thank you.'

I REMEMBER his gratitude in an interview with the SABC at the taxi rank in Mthatha the day after the tornado where he stated among other things in relation to his close protection team 'that their corpses would have carried him out of the pharmacy'.

Marieta van Wyk

I REMEMBER when President Mandela was elected in 1994 we, as the Presidency staff, were very concerned about our careers. On his first day Mary Mxadana arranged a meeting with him and all the staff. He welcomed all of us and said that he would not let us go but that he expected us to guide the incoming staff and work with them as a team. That speech meant a lot to us and we were so motivated and thankful for the meeting. It showed that he cared about us too.

I REMEMBER that I was involved with the refurbishment and redecoration of his suite of offices in the Union Buildings. It was a huge task involving the Public Works Department. When it was finalised he invited us for lunch at his residence, Mahlamba Ndlopfu, just to convey his appreciation. It was so amazing that he sat down to lunch with us and chatted with us.

I REMEMBER how sometimes when he was walking out with his bodyguards he would walk into my office, greet me by name and ask how I was doing. It showed how nice and sweet he was. Other presidents never greeted you. You had to stand still when they passed.

I REMEMBER that when there was going to be a meeting in the big room I would go and see if all the mics were ready. President Mandela would come in and give me a hug. It was really a very great honour to serve under him for five years, the highlight of my thirty-three years in government.

I REMEMBER Nelson Mandela as my hero and I salute him.

Zelda la Grange

I REMEMBER Madiba for the kind-hearted soul that he was.

I REMEMBER him for the authentic leader he was; how his principles and values were easy to emulate because he practiced them every day and that made them believable.

I REMEMBER him for being a pragmatist; in whose work logic and integrity took centre stage.

I REMEMBER a person who was unashamedly ethical.

I REMEMBER a dear, kind, loving, generous human being; someone who encouraged others to criticise him, for he knew that such criticism kept him humble and in touch with public sentiment.

I REMEMBER Madiba as the person who had the ability to listen to all views, free from any judgement and with the intent to truly understand another person's perspective.

I REMEMBER his crystal clear strategic mind and the revolutionary he was at heart.

I REMEMBER the husband, father and grandfather he was to his family and to me too, the most gentle, considerate grandpa.

I REMEMBER his infectious smile, the generosity in his eyes and how his support and strength encouraged me every day to keep going, despite the most difficult circumstances and relentless pressure.

I REMEMBER the Madiba who cared for us all with such an even hand.

I REMEMBER the warmth of his love, his consolation, his hope and most importantly believing that if he could touch one person's life every day, that he could change the world. And we all know he did.

Lawrence April

I REMEMBER when we were at Dullah Omar's funeral and there was a massive crowd. I was standing behind Madiba when someone tapped me on the shoulder. I turned around and it was a very old lady. She said, 'Please, Sir, I just want to touch him.' I stood aside and she touched Madiba. He looked at her and smiled. She had tears running down her face. It was so surreal, I remember going home and telling my wife it reminded me of the Biblical story of the woman touching the hem of Jesus' garment.

I REMEMBER being with him in Switzerland when the 2010 FIFA World Cup bid winner was announced. We knew we would win because we said we would not bring Madiba if we didn't get it. But the look of shock on his face was priceless when 'South Africa' was announced.

I REMEMBER that whenever he was going to visit someone, whether a president or a king, we knew that he would always take a turn from his path and go and greet the ordinary people. You couldn't blame people because they were so excited when they saw him. We basically had to protect him from people loving him to death.

I REMEMBER when we went on trips abroad with him we were treated like royalty. Before him and after him it was different.

I REMEMBER how some of the most famous people in the world, who were used to people wanting to be photographed with them, would line up to have their pictures taken with Madiba.

I REMEMBER when we were on our way somewhere and he would suddenly change the plan and have us go somewhere else, especially to visit sick people in hospital or at home. The look on people's faces was priceless when, without warning, this giant of a man suddenly appeared in front of them. What was always striking to me was that in those moments everyone present, from the lowliest worker to the top executive, were equal as he made no distinction.

I REMEMBER that when you brought him a newspaper, no one was allowed to have read it before him. If it looked like it had been read he would send you back to get another one. We would say, 'Whatever you do, don't touch the newspaper.'

I REMEMBER that wherever we drove you had to be familiar with the surroundings as he would always ask questions like, 'what is that mountain called?' or, 'what is the name of that building?'

I REMEMBER the genuine concern whether we as staff were given something to eat at dinner events and that he reprimanded his hosts when we said no.

Lizanne van Oudtshoorn-Richle

I REMEMBER that the first time I saw Mr Nelson Mandela in the flesh was at his inauguration as the president and I knew I wanted to be a part of it all.

I REMEMBER when the staff was called into the cabinet room to meet the new president in person, and what a moment it was when he greeted each staff member individually. He said he hoped we would be part of building the president's office and I remember thinking in amazement, 'Oh wow, he is asking us to be part of his office.'

I REMEMBER feeling immense excitement about working in President Nelson Mandela's office, after being unsure whether we would be given this opportunity.

I REMEMBER when one of his bodyguards peeked around my office door and told me to stay in my office. President Nelson Mandela then appeared in my office doorway and I did not quite know what to do and how to react. He asked me about my background and what I did in the office and then told me I am needed in the office to do this important job. At that moment I knew I would do anything for this man.

I REMEMBER, after a visit by President Robert Mugabe, Madiba walked with me from the entrance back to his office and explained the importance of respect and that one should handle it with care, but that it is also something to be earned.

I REMEMBER Madiba telling me in no uncertain terms, 'There is no such thing as African Time.'

I REMEMBER him speaking to me in Afrikaans when I had to end a meeting on time; especially if a guest had the feeling they had the right to his time.

I REMEMBER Madiba's excellent and mischievous sense of humour.

I REMEMBER a meeting with King Mswati III in Durban where Madiba asked the king for 25 cows for me and I asked why so little, to which he replied, 'Okay, I think 20 cows is enough, she is cheeky.'

I REMEMBER that looking for a husband for me became a pet joke of his and he asked President Museveni from Uganda, in front of a room filled with journalists, whether he has a husband for me and I almost melted into the floor.

I REMEMBER the way Madiba could spot people in a crowd to approach; it wasn't the loud person that pushed to the front.

I REMEMBER him speaking to an old Afrikaans lady in a crowd and how she said to me afterwards, 'Nou weet ek waarvan almal so praat, hy's 'n goeie mens.' [Now I know what everyone was talking about, he's a good person.]

I REMEMBER how he was always concerned about my safety and once when I was in the Richmond area before a visit to a mass funeral; he made the bodyguards promise him on the phone to look after me.

I REMEMBER how he made each and every state banquet a special occasion for our guests and the musicians when he danced to their last song.

I REMEMBER him introducing me to every head of state for whom I organised a state visit saying that I had done the hard work.

Jill Daniels

I REMEMBER one day the Old Man, as President Mandela was fondly called by his protectors, went to visit Number 2 Military hospital in Cape Town. At the end of the visit, the Old Man called me aside and pointed to a gentleman in the crowd. He then said, 'That man over there looks just like "your friend".' I didn't think the man looked like 'my friend' at all, but accepted that this was just his way of letting me know that he knew exactly what was going on without having to be told.

I REMEMBER that about two years later he stopped me at Parliament and said, 'Don't forget when "your friend" is ready to discuss lobola he needs to come and see me as I am your father too.'

Rory Steyn

I REMEMBER a state visit by the then president of Ghana, Mr Jerry Rawlings, in 1998 and the highly formal ceremony with a red carpet covering the driveway in front of the steps leading up to the Office of the President at the Union Buildings in Pretoria. There was a full military Guard of Honour drawn up in front of the red carpet, complete with a military band. A 21-gun salute was fired by a battery of four cannons from the nearby Thaba Tshwane or Voortrekkerhoogte to welcome the visiting head of state. There was the inevitable press platform behind the Guard of Honour, directly opposite the steps at the foot of which President Mandela awaited the arrival of President Rawlings. And when his motorcade arrived, it was escorted by a triangular configuration of military policemen dressed up in their finest, trying very hard not to fall off their motorcycles as they were only doing about 15 km/h, and wobbling all over the place! The door to President Rawlings's vehicle was opened by an *aide-de-camp*, a colonel dressed in full military uniform wearing white gloves. The president stepped up onto the steps of the Union Buildings, his motorcade pulled away and he turned to stand shoulder-to-shoulder with President Mandela facing the Guard of Honour. The national anthems of Ghana and South Africa were played, the

21-gun salute was fired and then the commander of the Guard of Honour marched up to President Rawlings, saluted him with his sabre and invited him to inspect the Guard of Honour.

I REMEMBER that the chief of protocol, the late John Reinders, had to request their Excellencies to accompany him into the president's office for tea and some *tête-à-tête* and on the way in, President Mandela would introduce to him members of his Cabinet lined up on the steps. Throughout the proceedings, I was positioned on a small ledge behind a pillar supporting the *porte-cochère* over the steps, no more than an arm's length from President Mandela's back. Ready to move from my concealed spot behind the pillar, next to a pot plant, I was very surprised to hear at such a formal occasion Madiba say to John Reinders, 'John, roep daardie kind!' [John, call that child.] And he pointed across the road to a spot next to the press stand. John looked up at me, I shrugged my shoulders and he said, 'Excuse me, Mr President?' Madiba pointed again and said to John, 'Call that child!' John dutifully went down the steps, across the red carpet, wound his way through an equally confused-looking detachment of soldiers in the Guard of Honour, and called the child over. He was standing right next to the press stand, an Afrikaans kid about 11 years old, dressed in his school tracksuit at 11 o'clock on a Tuesday morning. The child followed John Reinders through the Guard of Honour, across the red carpet and up onto the steps. We were all transfixed by what we saw. Madiba bent down and asked the child his name. Then to everyone's amazement, Madiba turned to his guest and said to the child, 'And this is President Rawlings of Ghana.' The little boy tentatively extended his hand and to his credit President Rawlings, who is a very impressive, regal man, a former Ghanaian Air Force pilot, bent down, shook hands with the child and rubbed his head. I swallowed quite hard on the lump that had by now formed in my throat as the symbolism of this unexpected encounter struck me. It was more than one black president calling a little white kid over to introduce him to another black president. It spoke powerfully of Madiba's humanity — the importance of the formal occasion didn't matter, the Cabinet ministers lined up on the steps going up to the Presidency could wait; this was simply an opportunity to introduce a child to his guest.

I REMEMBER thinking you cannot give training for that; people like Madiba are *born* with the common touch.

I REMEMBER accompanying President Mandela on his hugely successful state visit to the United Kingdom in July 1996, where Her Majesty Queen Elizabeth II hosted him at Buckingham Palace. The Queen placed a suite of rooms on the ground floor of the palace, called the Belgian Suite, at the president's disposal and Madiba was most intrigued by the three servants assigned to take care of his needs during his stay. There was a valet, a footman and a butler — all beautifully attired in their pinstriped trousers, starched white shirts and long grey tailcoats. The president told his private secretary, the late Mary Mxadana, on the last morning of the state visit that he'd like to take a photo with those servants that afternoon when we returned to the Belgian Suite before we departed. Mary duly passed on the message to the Master of the Household, who was a retired major-general from the British Army who had 600 palace staff 'under his command' as it were. That afternoon as we arrived back in the president's suite after a long day — in fact it had been a long four days — Madiba was tired. Suddenly the general appeared in the suite and announced that, 'We are ready for the photograph, sir.' The South African contingent (Madiba, his daughter Zenani, Sis Mary, Ashwyn and I) looked at one another, masking our surprise and communicating non-verbally, 'Let's see where this goes.' President Mandela asked, 'What would you like me to do, General?' To which the Master of the Household replied, 'Well follow me, sir.' He marched out of the Belgian Suite onto the lawn of Buckingham Palace with the president at his shoulder and all of us in tow. Around the corner we went, to be confronted by a huge scaffolding that the Brits had erected on the lawn of the palace, six or seven tiers high, where the entire staff of Buckingham Palace were arranged as only the British could do: tallest in the middle cascading to the shortest on either side on each of the rows, with two places in the centre of the bottom row on ground level. The general indicated the two spaces, asked Madiba to stand in one of them beside him, proudly puffed out his chest, and 'click', 'flash' went the official photographer and the moment was captured. When we arrived back in the Belgian Suite, Madiba thanked the general for the hospitality shown towards all of us; the general wished him a safe trip home and took his leave.

I REMEMBER the president then asking us, 'Does anybody have a camera?' Either Zenani or Sis Mary produced a small 'mik en druk' [point and shoot] camera from a handbag and the President said, 'Just call those three chaps please' — referring to the butler, the valet and the footman — 'because that's who I want a photo with.'

I REMEMBER thinking, 'That's probably never before happened in the long history of state visits to Buckingham Palace, nor since!'

Jerome Hardenberg

I REMEMBER when I did the planning for a visit to Upington after the election. It was an extremely conservative town. On the day that Mr Mandela arrived, there was a red carpet from the plane to the terminal and obviously there was an order of proceedings, protocol, somebody meets him and to the one side a lot of white policemen stood. They wanted nothing to do with this event. Mr Mandela was greeted and walked on the red carpet and then he noticed the group of policemen standing to the one side. He broke protocol, got off the red carpet and walked to the policemen. I was walking behind so I heard everything. He walked to them and he introduced himself. He said, 'Hi, I'm Nelson Mandela, what's your name?' So and so, 'Are you married?' Yes. 'Do you have children? Well, thank you for being here.' And he went through the same process, there were about six of them. He turned them around completely, absolutely. When he stepped away, I heard them swearing; I can't repeat what they said, but it was actually like saying, you know, 'Damn, PW was here before, he never did anything like this. This guy is amazing.' Just by going to greet them he had turned them and their attitudes. For me it was something absolutely amazing.

I remember we had a chopper visit to Qunu when he went to visit some people. The chopper was parked at some place and he walked over to speak to the people, obviously. He shook hands. There was a small woman, she was a little bit disabled and she couldn't get to Mr Mandela and was pressed up against the wire fence. He spoke to the people and shook hands and he started to walk back to the chopper. Before he boarded he looked over and he saw this woman being pressed up against the wire and he got off. He came back and he said, 'Ask that woman to come around here.' And they went around the fence, took her from outside the crowd and he spent some time with her.

I remember we had a five-hour walk with Madiba once in Qunu. We left the house at a quarter past six, and we got back at about quarter past eleven walking through the villages. It was amazing to see that somebody of his age could walk the way he walked, all the time interacting with the villagers. He didn't want the police vehicle close but we had to obviously hide it in case something went wrong, you know? We had to be available. He just said, 'Send the car home.' But we couldn't. If something went wrong we had to have the vehicle so we had to try to obscure the vehicle somehow.

I remember when we went to St Lucia in the Caribbean, to the Caricom conference, for the heads of state of all the different Caribbean countries. We got to the venue and I think the thing was supposed to start at about eleven. We got there just before half past ten. The other heads of state pitched up at a quarter past eleven, twenty past eleven. When they were all there Mr Mandela got the floor and he gave them a dressing down. He said, 'You guys are leaders, you must set an example.' And they sat listening to him, you know, like a dad who is talking to his kids. It was amazing for me to see that he set such a good example.

I REMEMBER if he decided he wants to walk then he wants to walk. He didn't have a shred of fear. No fear whatsoever.

I REMEMBER that the preferred time for his walks from his Cape Town residence, Genadendal was five o'clock, so we had to be there at about a quarter to, twenty to five to walk with him. But he was naughty sometimes — before we arrived, he would go and walk and the uniformed police would have to join him and we'd have to try to catch up and find out where he is. There were hardly any other people on the road. Sometimes when we were walking in the dark we would see ladies plying their business and we would try to get them to cross the road and walk on the other side. He would say, 'No no no, don't do that.' And he would shake their hands. 'How are you?' They were obviously elated. It was amazing.

I REMEMBER the tornado when we were in the pharmacy to buy soap one December. It took out the whole front of the chemist, blew it all down. I got something like six stitches in my foot because I tried to push some people away from the glass and it sounded like an explosion when it fell. Some of the protectors shielded Mr Mandela and you could see poles coming down, walls coming down. The guys in the armoured car, which weighed about three-and-a-half tonnes, said it felt like it was going to lift off the ground. He reacted very well. He was concerned obviously for the safety of the people and we had to get the general in charge as we had to find out — what we call in the police a 'sit-rep' — what the situation was; what type of damage was experienced, if any people were injured. We had to try and duck and dive and get a route back to Qunu that we assumed the tornado had already been through.

I REMEMBER when we were in Genadendal, he stayed home one day — it was myself, a guy by the name of Hein Bezuidenhout, our commander at the time, and Marcus Griebelaar his driver. Our birthdays were a day or two apart, the three of us and we decided to have a braai and we had this ingenious idea of inviting him to come and eat something with us. He came out from the house, whatever he was busy with he stopped, came outside and had some braai. We set a table for him and he sat down with us. We served him and each of us took individual photos with him and we had a group photo. That was very special for us.

Ryno Gouws

I REMEMBER one autumn morning in 1995 at Mr Mandela's house in Houghton, Johannesburg. It was a windy Saturday and the leaves of at least half a tree were dancing around the spotless cars we had just cleaned, ready to depart. I was standing chatting with Piet Irvia, when the front door of the house opened. It was Tata and I could tell that he had just woken up and wanted to check the weather before his day started. He made himself visible for a few seconds and retreated back into the house. Tata resurfaced about three minutes later, dressed in fluffy slippers and a bath robe, with a broom in his hand. He gave us a friendly greeting and started sweeping the driveway. We were all stunned and didn't really know what to do. I immediately froze and stood in admiration, watching the great Nelson Mandela sweeping the driveway.

I REMEMBER that a blue-uniformed policeman, armed with an R5 rifle, moved closer and I could see him behind Tata. My jaw dropped at the sight of a rare snapshot in history. I was looking at an armed white policeman in uniform, watching over Nelson Mandela, while he was sweeping and it suddenly came to me. Just a few years before, he had also worked under supervision and was watched for a different reason. At that moment, a duplicate image told a different story. It was a clear reminder of how far we had come, simply because one man decided not to sweep inequity under the rug.

Hayley Jacobs (née Lyners)

I REMEMBER Mr Mandela with the same love and fondness as that for my own grandfather. I remember his kindness, his compassion, his sternness and his sense of humour.

I REMEMBER being one of the few who called him 'Sir'. Mr Mandela rendered me speechless, completely and utterly, by his mere presence, to which he took great delight at times. I would freeze, and manage out of reverence to produce an audible greeting and thereafter would generally be at a loss for words.

I REMEMBER in December 2000 I was part of Mr Mandela's delegation to Paris, to conclude the signing of the Burundi Peace Agreement. We had been invited by our ambassador to visit the South African Embassy there as part of our tour. Upon our arrival we were welcomed by the entire staff contingency in the foyer of the embassy. Mr Mandela offered greetings and without missing a beat turned to his left, where I was standing and announced that I would be saying a few words on behalf of our delegation. To this day I cannot recall what I said or for how long I spoke, but I do remember Zelda's muffled laughter and Mr Mandela's amused smile.

I REMEMBER in 2002, after an emergency spinal operation, receiving a call from Mr Mandela. He asked whether I had been given exercises to do and whether I was doing them. Then he added that he was coming to visit me. A few days later, he arrived at my family home. I ushered Mr Mandela to the lounge area, he sat down and I stood close by, as I was not allowed to sit. Mr Mandela asked me whether I could sit. I said I shouldn't and he promptly marched me off to my room to make me lie down while he sat at my bedside explaining the importance of the exercises I should do and also demonstrated some moves that might be useful to me. Upon his departure, our street was filled with neighbours who had seen him arrive and the man I always called 'Sir' took the time to greet each and every one of them.

Desmond van Rooyen

I REMEMBER the first time I was nominated to be the Number One bodyguard. I travelled with Madiba in the main vehicle, from Houghton to the Union Buildings. During the trip, he tapped me on the shoulder and handed me his mobile phone. I took the phone from him. Madiba then asked me to please phone 'Bill' for him. I asked him, 'Which Bill sir'? And he replied 'Bill Clinton.' I was astounded, but I was able to call the White House and link President Clinton with President Mandela.

I REMEMBER when Madiba was discharged from Milpark Hospital after a knee operation. We arrived at his residence in Houghton for the drop off. When he opened the door everyone was looking at each other and at the same time Madiba was looking at us. He could not walk up the steps to the main door, let alone the small stairway to his bedroom on the first floor of his house. I was then instructed to assist one of my colleagues to carry the president up all the steps to his room. I was worried that we might drop Madiba going up the narrow stairs of the old house. I breathed a sigh of relief when we reached his bedroom on the first floor. I will never forget the smile on Madiba's face as he looked at my stressed face.

I REMEMBER the day in New York City, when we travelled with a Secret Service convoy to the Heads of State opening plenary for the 50th anniversary celebration of the United Nations. We drove through the busy streets of Manhattan, and as we moved closer to the UN headquarters, our convoy came to an abrupt stop and we could not move any further. The street crossing our convoy's path was barricaded by the NYPD. The Secret Service detail leader informed the South African close protectors that President Clinton's convoy was headed to the UN at the same time and that we had no choice but to wait for the street to reopen after his convoy passed. This message was relayed to Madiba who decided that if this was the case then he wanted to walk to the UN building. Madiba asked, 'How far is the UN building from us, chaps?' We told him it was around four street blocks. Madiba got out of the main vehicle and we started walking down the closed-off streets towards the UN headquarters. Police officers were lining the barriers to keep the thousands of people out of the street. The crowd started chanting, 'NELSON! NELSON! NELSON!' I watched Madiba wave to the chanting crowd and I thought about how privileged I was to be working with him. It was a tremendous experience to be part of the 'long walk to the UN'. Madiba stole the show that day.

I REMEMBER the day Mr Mandela spoke to me in Afrikaans and I replied in English. He kept addressing me in Afrikaans and I kept responding in English. Madiba was quiet for a while, before politely telling me that when he addresses me in my home language of Afrikaans he would expect me to answer him in Afrikaans. I never forgot this lesson and most of our informal conversations after this day were held in Afrikaans.

I REMEMBER the 4:30 am daily walks in the middle of winter in Johannesburg and Cape Town. The security team stationed at Madiba's house would sometimes wish that Madiba would oversleep or decide not to take the walk. Our wishes were very seldom fulfilled as Madiba often came out of the house, early in the morning, with a big smile. He would greet us warmly and then we were off into the cold, dark and empty streets of Cape Town or Johannesburg.

I REMEMBER walking onto the Ellis Park rugby pitch with Mr Mandela right before the kick-off of the 1995 Rugby World Cup. The atmosphere in the stadium was electric, the venue was packed to capacity with 65 000 people crammed into every seat that was available. There was a deafening noise in the stadium and the close protectors on the field had difficulty hearing the security conversations on our handheld radio ear pieces. Mr Mandela entered the pitch wearing the Springbok Captain Francois Pienaar's number 6 jersey. He immediately captured the attention of the crowd. And a small section on the main pavilion began chanting 'Nelson! Nelson!' The chanting spread through the stadium like a wave. I felt the adrenaline starting to pump through my veins. I have never experienced such a tremendous feeling of pride to be a South African, part of the rainbow nation, than in that moment. I thought to myself that this man could move mountains if he really wanted to.

Elzette Botha

I REMEMBER when President Mandela asked me to go and buy him some Dawn moisturising cream at the supermarket. He gave me a R100 note and asked if it would be enough to buy the cream. It made me realise how he has missed out on so many things in his life. My heart went out to him and I wanted to buy him several more bottles so that he could spoil himself a little bit.

I REMEMBER Christmas in his childhood village of Qunu when he hosted parties for all the kids. Oh, how their faces would just light up when they saw Santa and all the gifts! Among the special moments were President Mandela's smile and happiness when he was among the kids and how he spoke to them and sang: 'Twinkle Twinkle Little Star.'

I REMEMBER how he treated me as a lady on the team — always respectful and considerate. He always had time to stop and take my hand and see how I was doing. He once even introduced me to the Saudi delegation that visited South Africa as a female protector who was part of his team.

I REMEMBER the life lessons he taught me: To be respectful and treat all people equally. He would stop and speak to the guy who swept the street and when waitresses would serve him his food he would look up and say, 'Thank you'. I still follow his example today and make it a point to acknowledge someone who might have a junior position. As the saying goes, 'Be kind to the one below you, he might just pass you on his way up.'

I REMEMBER when he always said to never forget your roots and where you come from! Don't ever forget your origin, but don't let your past be the compass of your future.

I REMEMBER the year after my husband, Riaan Smuts, and I left the Presidential protection team in 2000 and moved to the Middle East, President Mandela invited us to have tea with him when he visited Sharjah.

I REMEMBER when President Mandela signed my letter of reference and a photo of himself. These items are part of the most precious items in my home. I have his photo in my office and am so thankful for the time I served on his protection team and the life lessons I have learnt from him.

Tania Bagley

I REMEMBER that I completed some typing for Madiba's PA, Mary Mxadana, and upon completion she asked me how she may repay my kind assistance. Working in the Office of the President one doesn't often get to meet or speak with Madiba even though we were a close-knit staff. So without a moment's hesitation I requested a one-on-one meeting with Madiba. I was not sure where that courage came from but it was arranged immediately. On the actual day it happened, I felt a range of emotions from absolute terror to extreme excitement. I thought out exactly what I was going to say but oh what a foolish thought that was. When Mr Mandela stepped into the room all thought flew out the door. I was speechless and immobile. He filled the room with a presence unlike any other and seemed to dwarf over me in such an unthreatening manner. I then realised just how tall he really was. He took my hand and I introduced myself and the manager I work for in his office. He had a deep timbre to his voice and a kindness in his eyes which is indelibly imprinted in my mind.

I REMEMBER that he replied, 'I had no idea I had such beautiful ladies working in my office' and smiled. A few other things were said but at that stage I ceased to hear anything as time stood still. I was totally overwhelmed. It was a moment in my life I will never forget and how honoured, humbled and blessed I feel for having worked in the Office of the President, or the Presidency as it was later called.

Marius Visser

I REMEMBER the first time I met Mr Mandela he was at the Union Buildings for an appointment with President FW de Klerk. I was a plain-clothes policeman in charge of the president's office and I was very impressed with him being so different to the propaganda we had been taught. He greeted me warmly and we had a whole conversation in my language, Afrikaans. He was very sincere and that experience really changed my whole mind-set.

I REMEMBER that after the election I was based at the president's office (Union Buildings) working with the close protection team. We were called into a meeting by the senior bodyguard to Mr de Klerk who asked us who wanted to go with Mr de Klerk and who wanted to stay with President Mandela. Without hesitation I said I would stay.

I REMEMBER that the day he started work the office was in shambles. When President Mandela came in there was nothing. We had to get Foreign Affairs to set it up. He came in and greeted each and every person with a handshake and told us that he appreciated what we did and that he was looking forward to working with us.

I REMEMBER watching him on the CCTV as he arrived for work and left. Never once did I see him walk past a cleaner and not greet them. There was not a night that he walked to his car without greeting everyone he encountered.

I REMEMBER on his first birthday as president, there were a lot of big cakes in the office. He said we should divide the cakes up so that there would be a slice for every person who worked at the Union Buildings.

I REMEMBER when his office phone was not working and we got Telkom in to fix it. Normally intelligence would have had to first sweep and debug the room. President Mandela, who was reading the newspaper at his desk, excused himself and moved from his desk to let the technician do his work.

I REMEMBER that he always insisted that his personal chef cook for the bodyguards on duty.

I REMEMBER that he increased the number of close protection staff so that they could have breaks and time off to spend with their families.

Etienne van Eck

I REMEMBER meeting President Mandela in 1991 at the CODESA multi-party talks. I was twenty-five and the co-commander of the security contingent responsible for securing the talks. One day when all the leaders were at the World Trade Centre in Kempton Park I got a CODESA poster and went to the ANC offices and asked if Mandela would sign it for me. He did. I then went to the offices of the National Party, and asked De Klerk's bodyguards if he would sign it. I knew them because we were all part of the SAP's national VIP/special guard unit. They were agreeable, but when they saw Mandela had already signed it, they had their doubts as to whether De Klerk would sign AFTER Mandela (De Klerk was still the president). So we devised a plan to cover Mandela's signature. The poster was rolled up, so we unrolled it, and put books on it to flatten it out, conveniently covering Mandela's signature. And De Klerk signed it, in the 'O' of CODESA.

I REMEMBER when Madiba insisted on going out himself to buy flowers for his secretary on Secretary's Day.

I REMEMBER when Madiba was courting Graça Machel. He walked her home, down the middle of the street. He'd take her hand and we, the protectors, just tried to melt away.

I REMEMBER when Madiba told me I had the courage to turn tragedy into triumph.

Tania Arrison

I REMEMBER first meeting President Mandela when I worked at the Presidency in 1994. It was a truly humbling experience. This iconic man, yet so humble and gentle in stature, reassuring us as staff members that it would be a difficult period of adjustment, yet given time and effort we would get through it.

I REMEMBER that although Madiba did not speak about his faith or religious affiliation, he was a man of great faith. He was keenly aware of how apartheid had been supported by various churches and he had made it his life's work to reconcile and unite people across race, gender and even religion.

I REMEMBER that Madiba continuously admitted his own imperfections, sometimes in very public arenas, by stating that he was not a saint, unless one thinks of a saint as a sinner who keeps on trying. Madiba surrounded himself with men and women of integrity, no matter their race or political affiliation. His goal was to bring about healing and reconciliation.

I REMEMBER the day when Prof Gerwel facilitated a meeting about Madiba's last will and testament where his lawyers discussed some of his amendments. As changes were made, I printed them and I was blown away by the generosity of this iconic leader, who had even made provision for schools, and his personal assistant!

I REMEMBER the day my daughters and my mom met Mr Mandela. They were amazed by his gentle nature. One of my daughters was wearing a bracelet she had bought a few days earlier and Madiba took such a keen interest in it while holding her hand and wanted to know more about it. The absolute adoration that shone from his face was not forced, not pretentious, but absolutely genuine. She went on to explain to him that she had bought the bracelet from a street vendor. He chuckled and said that she should continue supporting small business! In that moment, he had made such an indelible impression on my eldest daughter that she wanted to know more about this man, this great leader who people all around the world revered. She went on to study his life and times, and is currently studying law and politics at the University of Pretoria. She plans to continue with her LLB, to honour Madiba's life and to a certain extent follow his example.

Gert 'Barries' Barnard

I REMEMBER in one of the defining moments of his presidency, Madiba appeared at the final of the 1995 Rugby World Cup at Ellis Park Stadium in Johannesburg where South Africa triumphed against their old rivals, New Zealand. On that day Madiba made rugby into a sport for all South Africans. I watched as Madiba, dressed in the number 6 rugby shirt of the South African captain, Francois Pienaar, walked onto the field before the match. For a moment the thousands of rugby fans stood in dumb disbelieving silence. Someone took up a cry that others followed, 'Nel-son, Nel-son', which grew louder and louder and ended in a thundering roar like an African lion. I was standing behind one of the proudest presidents the world has ever seen when Madiba handed the trophy to our victorious captain. And it was one of the proudest moments in the history of South Africa and certainly the most humble of my career as a bodyguard in the Presidential Protection Unit of the South African Police Service.

I REMEMBER the great honour of protecting an international icon and statesman and a servant of the people of our beautiful and diverse country.

I REMEMBER that after I left the police force and stopped protecting Madiba, I was assigned to Paul Hewson, aka Bono, of the rock band U2. He and his family were visiting South Africa and they visited Madiba at the Nelson Mandela Foundation in Johannesburg.

I REMEMBER at the end of the visit, Zelda la Grange, Madiba's personal assistant, asked me if I want to greet Madiba. I replied that it would be good to see him again. Zelda reminded Madiba that I was one of the bodyguards protecting him during his term as President of South Africa. Madiba replied, 'I remember you, but do you remember me?' I laughed and replied, 'Who can ever forget you, Mr President.'

Tasneem Carrim

I REMEMBER that while I was just a junior researcher in Madiba's communications unit, he really listened to everybody's views. He read every single little thing in the briefing notes we sent him. No item was too small or insignificant for him. More importantly, he took action immediately even if just to respond to minor issues we raised in the briefing notes. In one instance, he diverted his motorcade to meet with a community of retrenched workers because he had read about the recent retrenchments in my briefing note.

I REMEMBER that in 1996 he travelled to KwaZulu-Natal where there was still a high level of political violence. He said he wanted to again call on people to throw their weapons into the sea but he wanted to say it in isiZulu and he wanted it to be in perfect language. We drafted it and he delivered the speech beautifully.

I REMEMBER during the negotiations for a new constitution and particularly regarding labour and the right to strike, Madiba met with business leaders who wanted to be able to lock out striking workers. When he came out of the meeting he expressed to the media the view of business.

I REMEMBER that a friend of mine, Kenneth Creamer, who worked at Cosatu, was concerned about this and told me he had written a paper that he wished he could share with Tata. At that moment Madiba came out of a meeting and I grabbed Kenneth's hand and introduced him to Madiba. After they chatted Madiba said he had been very convincing and their chat had helped him to change his views on the lock-out clause.

I REMEMBER when I used to travel with Madiba on some international trips and he would often ask dignitaries in my presence if they would help to find me a husband. These include the Pope, Fidel Castro and Gro Harlem Brundtland.

I REMEMBER all the secrecy around Madiba and Mrs Machel's wedding in 1998. His spokesperson, Parks Mankahlana, was severely criticised by journalists for 'lying' to them about it. Soon thereafter, at a press conference in Brazil, Madiba asked me to gather the South African journalists. He told them he had read their comments about Parks and said they were wrong. He said if there was anyone to blame it was Madiba himself as he had instructed Parks to keep the event a secret.

I REMEMBER when we were just starting to get email and the internet, I went on an internet research course and Madiba asked if I could show him what I had learnt. I went to his house to discover that he needed very basic lessons. How to open and send emails, for instance. I called my brother Farouk to say we would be sending him an email and that he must reply immediately. Madiba typed a short email saying 'hello' and asking how he was and then signed it 'Nelson'. A few minutes later a very shocked reply came back from my brother.

I REMEMBER being in charge of Madiba's farewell dinner when he stepped down as president, for all his staff from the Cape Town and Pretoria offices. Everyone from cleaners to administration staff were invited to the event at the Indaba Hotel in Fourways. We played a Miriam Makeba song called 'Aluta Continua' and at the start of the song the junior staff was encouraged to ask Madiba and Mrs Machel and other senior people to dance. Madiba yelled, 'Put it louder! Put it louder!' as he danced away with a junior staff member from the Finance Department.

Loïs Dippenaar

I REMEMBER how I felt the first time Madiba called me by my name.

I REMEMBER a short trip to Zimbabwe when Madiba was invited to address the World Council of Churches in Harare in December 1998. On our way there, he called me to the front of the plane. As always, I had a notebook ready to take notes of whatever it was that he wanted us to attend to when we got back home. He said I could put the notebook away and asked about the wellbeing of my parents, my husband and daughter, and then he took my one hand and said: 'Loïs, you mustn't be ashamed of your people. The Afrikaner has much to be proud of and has a very valuable role to play in rebuilding our country.' How did he know about my inner struggles and confusion?

I REMEMBER Madiba's last breakfast in Genadendal. Prof Gerwel, Zelda and I joined him and he was so relaxed. Madiba told one story after the other, stories that we all knew very well. His recollections of those stories never changed and he predictably laughed at certain places. And it felt good. And safe.

I REMEMBER how perplexed I was after the birth of our daughter when so many hospital staff members popped in to greet me. Eventually, one of the nurses explained that they just wanted to see who the woman was who had received flowers from Nelson Mandela.

I REMEMBER how, on a state visit to Hungary, it seemed as if every person we met in Budapest explained to us that the city consisted of two parts: Buda and Pest. It became the topic of many a joke among the staff and Prof Gerwel must have shared this with Madiba, because on the second day, on our way from the Buda side of the city, Madiba called from his cellphone (he was a few cars ahead of me in the motorcade) to say that he had just crossed the Danube River and that he was pleased to report that the weather in Pest was lovely.

I REMEMBER that on Red Nose Day in 1998 Madiba couldn't finish his speech at an event in Toronto, Canada. It was a long day and he was feeling lightheaded and was about to faint. He was scheduled to fly back home that evening and we all accompanied him to the airport. Before he got onto the plane he walked around greeting each one of us. He told me not to worry and gave me a hug. I kept worrying. We all did. He was our anchor.

I REMEMBER the joy on Madiba's face when he sang 'Twinkle Twinkle Little Star' with children in different parts of the world.

Vimla Naidoo

I REMEMBER the first time I met Madiba. It was in September 1995, my second day at Protocol in the Office of the President. The department was a flurry of activity in preparing for a reception for His Holiness Pope John Paul II. After the reception, Madiba invited all his guests to greet His Holiness and the chief of protocol, John Reinders, asked staff to also join the queue. I was elated and could hardly believe I was going to greet Madiba in person. As I drew closer to Madiba, I couldn't stop smiling. When it was my turn, I marched confidently up to him, my hand outstretched, ready to greet him, and that's when Madiba smiled and asked me, 'Aren't you going to greet the Pope?' I was so focused on Madiba that I had walked right past the Pope! I hurriedly turned back and the Pope said, 'Bless you, child.' In a matter of seconds I was standing in front of Madiba again. His endearing smile helped lessen my utter despair at my *faux pa*s, and then he asked me a few questions and teased me, asking why I'm not still at school.

I REMEMBER stories Madiba loved to share — of his days as a young boy, of mischief and adventure and then the stories of prison, of hardship and camaraderie — and even though we'd heard them a few times, we never tired of Madiba relating them, in a way only he could. I feel privileged and honoured to have heard these snippets of history in Madiba's voice.

I REMEMBER Madiba's sense of humour. One morning at the office, I presented him with some letters to sign. He took out his fountain pen, which staff had aptly named the 'Presidential Pen' because this was the one he preferred to use for signing. We were not too fond of this pen, as it was sometimes prone to smudging. Madiba asked to test it on some paper and I passed him my notebook. He wrote something and, satisfied that the pen would pose no problems that morning, he began signing the letters. Once we were done, I glanced at my notebook, and saw Madiba had written, 'Vimla is tall'. I said to him, 'Tata, it isn't nice to make fun of the vertically challenged' and he erupted in laughter.

I REMEMBER Madiba's genuine care and concern, and the loyalty it inspired in his staff. Madiba saw you — he knew the name of your spouse, your children and never failed to ask after them.

Ella Govender

I REMEMBER getting a job at the Office of the President because Madiba wanted an Indian woman to manage his official residence in Cape Town. I joined the staff of Genadendal in 1995. A few months later I was appointed to manage all the official residences in South Africa.

I REMEMBER Madiba for the very special person he was. Shortly after our first meeting and interaction it didn't seem like we had an employee and statesman relationship. He immediately put me at ease. He often referred to me as his 'boss' although he was mine.

I REMEMBER that he insisted on meeting my family and inviting them over for dinner with him and maintained a relationship with them over the years.

I REMEMBER that he was someone of great integrity, immense stature, humility and selflessness.

I REMEMBER the great lesson I learnt from him was his respect for all people regardless of their colour, creed or social standing.

I REMEMBER Madiba's spirit of adventure and his great sense of humour.

I REMEMBER his astonishing memory of things past and present. He would ask me to call someone for him, and automatically provide their telephone number himself.

I REMEMBER how his love for children was his positive weakness.

I REMEMBER how Madiba taught me to be thankful for my mistakes as 'they teach you valuable lessons' and to tackle each new challenge 'because it will build your strength and character'.

I REMEMBER that he would say that you gain strength, courage and confidence from each of life's experiences.

Maeline Engelbrecht

I REMEMBER standing in the foyer of Hotel de Paris in Monte Carlo waiting for Madiba and Mum to arrive, and as they entered the hotel, Madiba came straight to me and said: 'Maeline you are here, now I feel at home!'

I REMEMBER the send-off from Durban harbour when the *QE2* was once again in South African waters but this time as a cruise liner. Almost the entire population of KwaZulu-Natal descended on the harbour to see Madiba and Mum on the deck of the majestic *QE2*, waving at the crowd, with balloons and streamers flying in the sky and cars blowing their horns to bid them well on their voyage.

I REMEMBER in 2001 when Radio 702 broke a world record for a giant flower arrangement to wish Madiba well following his treatment for prostate cancer. In the atrium of Sandton City shopping mall, supporters came and placed flowers on a specially designed flower structure that contained 40 000 flowers, and stood 6.5 metres high and 3.75 metres wide. It required 20 metres of steel, 2 000 litres of water, 5 000 cable ties, 300 steel clamps, 140 square metres of flower foam and 900 plastic buckets. Madiba invited the 702 crew to the office and via a live broadcast thanked them and everyone for buying flowers to make up the biggest bouquet of flowers in the world!

I REMEMBER taking the staff of Radio 702 to Madiba's office (which was still at the house on 13th Avenue, Houghton) as Madiba wanted to thank them for the initiative and for wishing him a speedy recovery. I got a nice kiss before proceedings started live on Radio 702.

I REMEMBER being at Madiba's residence with Achmat Dangor and Sibongile Mkhabela and Madiba told us a joke about a man based abroad who contacted him to convince him that he had billions of dollars to donate to the Children's Fund but all he needed was for Madiba to purchase his ticket to South Africa. I burst out laughing, while Achmat and Bongi still had a serious look on their faces — Madiba nudged me with his arm and gestured towards them saying: 'They didn't catch the joke!'

I REMEMBER being in Tromsø, Norway before the 46664 Arctic concert. Zelda asked me to sit with Madiba and keep him company while she ran a few errands. Madiba sat by the window reading his South African newspapers that the office used to send him while he was travelling abroad, and I sat on the couch next to him working on my laptop. I recall closing my laptop to rather read, but as soon as I closed it, Madiba put down his newspapers and wanted to chat. We talked about my growing up in Butterworth in the Eastern Cape, and about my sisters, and of course he teased me about why he has never met my young man.

I REMEMBER Madiba's 91st birthday lunch at The Saxon. I took my sister, Heather, to meet Madiba and Mum for the first time. Madiba was very relaxed in his armchair and was nibbling on gooseberries as we chatted. He pulled my sister's arm to draw her closer so that he could kiss her — I remember her being totally taken in by Madiba and Mum — who wouldn't be?

I REMEMBER Madiba teasing me about boys and asking me, 'How many boyfriends do you have?' I gestured with my fingers to make a zero, and trust Madiba to notice the three fingers that were standing up, to which he exclaimed '*three* boyfriends!' I thought it was best just to let it go.

I REMEMBER when we were taking photographs of members of the Nelson Mandela Foundation's Investment Committee of which Tokyo Sexwale — 'Chief' as we called him — was the chairman. Madiba did not look too pleased with the whole situation, and his expression was captured in the first photo which I took with Chief's camera. Chief needed to save the situation quickly, and told me to go and stand by Madiba. When I walked towards Madiba, he stood up and smiled and the photo was taken, unfortunately minus Chief!

I REMEMBER Madiba and Mum always recognising their staff no matter what the occasion or where we were in the world, always with a kiss and sometimes even before greeting the dignitaries, and *always* demonstrating how thankful they were for the work we did for them.

Hermann 'Harry' Coetzee

I REMEMBER when we were in Mozambique for a long period of time and one day Madiba spoke to Rory Steyn, our team leader, and they were discussing that the plane would be coming to pick him up and take him to Cape Town. Rory then informed us that we could ask our partners to get on to the plane and join us.

I REMEMBER that Madiba did not only do that once. We had been in the Transkei for weeks and he once again agreed we put our wives on the plane. I had never heard of a leader anywhere in the world who would even think about doing something like that.

I REMEMBER once flying with him to Cape Town. We went to the naval base and got onto a naval ship. While we were out on the open sea the weather picked up and got a bit rough. A military vessel is built for speed not comfort and I was trying not to fall and at the same time to stop him from falling over.

I REMEMBER one day when were in an informal settlement, east of Johannesburg, where there was political unrest. We drove into the area and stopped; the next moment we could feel the ground trembling. Down the road came an impi – some in traditional Zulu gear with assegais and knobkerries.

I REMEMBER that the men stopped right in front of us, and Madiba walked into the group. They stopped dancing and singing and stood still and listened to him. He spoke to their leader and told them to stop the killings and he walked back to the car and we drove off. The men were still standing still when we left.

I REMEMBER that he would often say, 'I have got a job to do and you have got a job to do.' That day our team leader told him, 'Our job is to protect you.' Luckily everything worked out on that day.

I REMEMBER when we were in Canada and he did not feel well. We took him back to the hotel and had doctors examine him. The decision was made that he had to go back to South Africa as soon as possible. We were all a bit tense and worried. We knew the pilots had to have certain hours of continuous sleep before they could fly. But every so often someone would wake them and they would have to start those hours again. Eventually we said, 'Let the pilots sleep. They will fly when they can fly.'

I REMEMBER when we were in Libya; we had to land in Tunis and then drive him in a convoy from the border to Gaddafi's place. Gaddafi was well known for making long speeches so Madiba and Gaddafi agreed beforehand for Gaddafi not to speak for longer than I think it was twenty minutes. After their meeting Gaddafi spoke to the people. Not for longer than what was agreed. Then as we were about to leave Gaddafi wanted to meet with him again. He said he could not, so some of his men took our chief of protocol, John Reinders, into another room to negotiate. They must have thought that John would arrange for Madiba to come back. We went back into the palace and got John and then we could leave.

I REMEMBER Madiba loving children and always making time to stop and talk to them.

I REMEMBER Madiba treating every person with the same respect.

Des Chetty

I REMEMBER sometime around 1996 I was in the scout vehicle en route from Waterkloof Airforce Base to Houghton as we passed the Oliphantsfontein off-ramp on the N1 highway, and I received a call via radio from my colleague Sam Shitlabane saying, 'We are going to Sandton City, Tata wants a pen from CNA.' I replied, asking Sam to find out from Madiba what the pen looks like. I wanted us to buy it for him knowing what a scene he would cause by appearing at the mall. Sam exclaimed, 'Hey man Chetty, we are going to Sandton City – Tata wants to go!' When we got to the mall there was mass pandemonium of joy as people all around us were yelling, laughing and taking photos. It was crazy.

I REMEMBER in September 1997 I worked in the advance team in Switzerland where South Africa was bidding to host the 2004 Olympic Games in Cape Town. We stayed at the Dolder Grand Hotel in Zurich. Apparently the media had complained about our 'assertive posture' while looking after Madiba. We convened a meeting with Jason Tshabalala and as I walked through the Presidential Suite where Madiba was sitting quietly, he looked up and said, 'Aahh Chetty, you are here.' I said, 'Yes Tata.' He told us to be more polite and to smile at the press.

I REMEMBER in 2007 when we were in Plessislaer, a township close to Pietermaritzburg, where masses of people had congregated in a soccer field chanting and singing for Madiba. He was very upset as the pyramid barbed wire prevented children from trying to touch him.

I REMEMBER when we were touring the Eastern Cape where private sector companies were building schools and Madiba said to kids in the villages, that gone are the days where you can get by with matric. Today you need two to three degrees.

Wayne Hendricks

I REMEMBER when Madiba was in Venice, Italy and because I also came from the Eastern Cape, I was designated to make him pap in the mornings. I had to be in the kitchen of the five-star hotel every day at 5 am. One morning I burnt the pap due to my excessive espresso drinking and brushing up on Italian with my new-found Italian chef friends. We only had one packet of South African pap so I was forced to reluctantly take the burnt serving to Tata. He tasted it and said, 'Wayne, how do you make this so smoky? It is delicious.' So every morning going forward I burnt the pap.

I REMEMBER how, when reading a newspaper, Madiba was meticulous in the way he would fold it from one page to the other. Over the years I realised that it was about controlling the little things not about efficiency.

I REMEMBER the sadness in Madiba's eyes when someone close to him got hurt or was in distress.

I REMEMBER the absolute child-like joy when Madiba would interact with children or go for a walk in the veld in Qunu telling whoever was with us that day about his childhood.

I REMEMBER the smell of Madiba's cologne and how to this day it always lingers with me.

I REMEMBER the day we visited the Zimbabwe Ruins and while holding his hand we both slowly started slipping off a small but wet grass hill. While we held on tightly to each other's hands, Madiba quipped, 'Wayne, I think we are going to fall … let's make sure we smile for the cameras.'

Bakkies Breytenbach

I REMEMBER in 1990 I was working on the protection detail of President FW de Klerk as a very young naïve protection officer. One day we received notice that a guest was coming to Tuynhuys to visit the president, one Nelson Mandela from prison. I have to confess I'd heard that name once or twice in my life before and did not really know who this person was, except that he was from prison. Under great secrecy Mr Mandela arrived in the underground parking of Tuynhuys and I was there to receive him and make sure he went to the president's office. I greeted him, led the way to the staircase, made sure he went into the lift, and then quickly ran up the stairs to receive him upstairs again. He was surprised that I was there when he exited the lift. The same procedure followed when he departed. At the vehicle he stopped, turned around and said, 'Thank you very much.' He waved and got into the vehicle and departed. I did not fully realise that I was in the presence of such a great man. If I only had known then.

I REMEMBER that in 1996 when Deputy President De Klerk resigned I was transferred back to the Presidential Protection Unit as a planning officer and served in the protection details of President Mandela and Deputy

President Mbeki. The first operation I was assigned to plan and manage was the opening of a school somewhere in Giyani. After the landing of the Oryx and the welcoming party swarming to receive the president, the walkabout of the school started. We were not one minute into the walkabout when Mr Mandela stopped, I was a few steps ahead of him, and everyone stopped. As I turned around to see what the hold-up was, he called me closer and said, 'Oh, are you working for me now?' I replied, 'Yes, sir.' And he then said, 'I know where you have been working. You are welcome here,' and we continued. This was one of the greatest moments in my life. Mr Mandela did not care for who I worked previously, he just unconditionally welcomed me in his protecting team.

I REMEMBER being introduced by Mr Mandela to the president of Botswana, President Ketumile Masire in Botswana.

I REMEMBER being there when Mr Mandela met Muhammad Ali in New York.

I REMEMBER wearing the same suit, shirt and socks without a change of underwear for three days on the SA Navy boat the SAS *Outeniqua* in Pointe-Noire, Republic of the Congo when Mr Mandela brokered peace talks between Laurent Desire Kabila and Mobutu Sese Seko.

I REMEMBER travelling to the USA just after the Seattle riots when Mr Mandela met Bill Gates and I was introduced to Bill and Melinda Gates.

I REMEMBER Mr Mandela as one of the most amazing people I ever had the privilege to meet and work for.

Henk van Heerden

I REMEMBER driving a golf cart, carrying Madiba onto the field at Loftus Versfeld, the holy grail of rugby, when the Springboks played against Wales on 26 June 2004. As we entered the pitch the unsuspecting spectators exploded in joyful singing when they saw Madiba. We as protectors had to use hand signals to communicate with each other as clear radio communication through the earpieces became impossible. The Boks won the game 53–18.

I REMEMBER the friendly face of Madiba when I entered his hotel suite during foreign visits to escort the hotel staff to service his suite.

I REMEMBER the vast kilometres, early sunrise mornings and late sunset evenings through the beautiful country of South Africa providing technical support at venues in support of close protection operations attended by Madiba.

I REMEMBER Madiba asking about my family while we were on trips out of town or abroad. He would say, 'En hoe gaan dit by die huis?' [And how are things at home?]

I REMEMBER the day, in my capacity as a security advisor, I attended a security implementation meeting at Madiba's residence in Houghton, when Ms Meme Kgagara invited me to see Madiba and he congratulated me on my 40th birthday.

Conroy Herandien

I REMEMBER on the eve of the Millennium, Madiba was due to address the world from Robben Island. There was nothing on his programme for the afternoon so at about two o'clock he said he needed an atlas. We went to Cavendish Square mall on New Year's Eve in a very busy Cape Town. Everyone recognised him. There were literally thousands of people. We popped into a small bookshop in the mall for the atlas and at the till they asked for R825. He asked me to pay for it and I said, 'Tata, that's almost my monthly salary so I can't pay. We'll make arrangements for somebody to come and pay.' He knew he was causing chaos in the mall but he liked the crowd. It was almost like he needed to be among people.

I REMEMBER when Madiba went on a state visit to Indonesia in 1997 and some people were critical that he was to meet President Suharto, who was apparently a dictator. When we arrived in Jakarta we were ferried off to the presidential compound. By the late afternoon we had to join President Suharto at a banquet. I pulled out Madiba's chair next to President Suharto. They exchanged a few pleasantries but within five minutes Madiba told Suharto, 'I want to see Xanana Gusmao now,' referring to the jailed East Timor independence leader. Madiba insisted. He had, I think, a tooth-pick in his mouth and he was just sitting there. It was as if he froze, that he wanted his way immediately. Suharto then agreed and we rushed through the banquet. Lo and behold, about an hour later we heard this noise outside which sounded like a helicopter. I went onto the roof and ten identically dressed guys got off this military helicopter and one of them turns out to be Gusmao who went into Madiba's room.

I REMEMBER that we went with Madiba to Seattle in 1999 for an event for Bill Gates's father. We got invited for breakfast at Bill Gates's house, which is on Lake Washington. While we were there President Clinton called. He was going to Disney World with Elian Gonzales, this Cuban boy who was going to be repatriated to Cuba. He asked Madiba to join them there. I flew from Seattle to Miami and then to Orlando to go and prepare for Madiba's visit. The Secret Service met me at the airport and took me straight to a meeting because Clinton was arriving at the same time as Madiba. Clinton was scheduled to land an hour before Madiba. I don't know if it is Federal Law or something but the airspace should be cleared half an hour before and half an hour after Air Force One lands. Madiba's plane came in within that time and they made it circle. Wayne Hendricks contacted me from Madiba's plane. He said, 'Look, what's going on here?' I said, 'The Secret Service don't want you to touch down because it's their rules – the president lands, nobody else.' The radio went silent and then Wayne came back. 'Make sure President Clinton knows that Madiba was here. He's leaving now.' I went to Clinton's main guy and I said, 'Tell POTUS Madiba is leaving, he will refuel somewhere else and he's gone.' Five minutes later, Madiba's Gulf Stream pulls up next to Air Force One. They looked like Mother and Child on the tarmac.

I REMEMBER that we were invited to the Aspen Conference in Colorado. Madiba was on a panel to be interviewed by Christiane Amanpour from CNN and Charlie Rose. Charlie Rose started by asking him, 'How can you travel in such luxury while your people are suffering in townships?' They had to cut the feed the way Madiba went on with that guy. He said, 'Look at your projects.' I think the projects are their slums or something. Madiba was just furious. He stood his ground and he gave us confidence because you know as much as you focus on your job you are in awe of these people, rich people, famous people. It gives you confidence to do whatever you do.

I REMEMBER when there was a panic button in his bedroom so he could call the security at home if needs be. Every so often he would activate this device and we would respond within seconds by bursting into his room only to find him, in bed, with his hand outstretched greeting you in that distinctive voice, 'Yes. How are you?' After shaking his hand, we would ask why he had activated the alarm. Every single time he would apologise profusely and explain that he had activated it accidently. Strangely after Mum Graça moved in, no panic alarm was set off ever again.

I REMEMBER one day we took him home for lunch at his official Cape Town residence, Genadendal. He was received at the main entrance by Ella Govender and the chef Hilton Little. We dropped him at the front door and moved the convoy to our standby area in the shade. The driver of one of the lead vehicles did not see an obstacle in the driveway and just drove over it. Hysterical screams came from Kumalo, an old man from the housekeeping staff who was on his way with a knife to slaughter the chicken as Madiba wanted freshly slaughtered chicken for lunch. All that was left was a flat bundle of brown feathers and a solid egg that popped out when the chicken was run over. None of us had the courage to tell Madiba that we killed his lunch so we needed to find a live chicken in Cape Town within the hour. We activated everyone, even friends, to help look for a live chicken. We found a vendor of live chickens near Philippi and it was slaughtered just in time for his meal.

Piet Irvia

I REMEMBER the first time I was driving for him — from his residence to the Waterkloof Airforce Base. I am a smoker and I had a smoke just before we left his house. Almost as soon as he was in the car he said to me, 'Piet, where is that stompie?' From then on I didn't smoke for at least half an hour before we went somewhere and I always carried breath freshener with me.

I REMEMBER that Madiba always treated people with respect. I was with him when he met kings and queens, presidents and politicians, CEOs of companies and cleaners, and ordinary people. The way he talked and listened to all of them was the same. He met people, not their title or position.

I will never forget when Madiba met Mrs Machel. The way he walked, the way he talked when he was with her, the glitter in his eyes when he looked at her — it was brilliant. Whenever she went on trips by herself he wanted to fetch her at the airport and he wanted to go himself and buy her flowers; he would not send one of us.

I REMEMBER when we went abroad he insisted that we all have dinner together when possible. In Washington DC we stayed at Prince Bandar's guest house. We were all sitting at the dinner table with Madiba at the head, Mum next to him, Zelda on the other side next to Madiba and myself next to Mum and the doctor and other protectors completing the table. You have these guys walking around the table with all kinds of food and they dish up for you. The food was fantastic but you want to be prim and proper so you only took a spoon or so on your plate. Mum said to me, 'Piet, you are a big guy, why do you eat so little?' I replied 'No Mum, this is enough for me. I'm fine.' Madiba chipped in and said, 'Mum, do not be fooled by this. From here they will go and eat somewhere else.' He knew us so well.

Tau Thekiso

I REMEMBER when we attended a function for the anniversary of the assassination of Samora Machel in Xilembene in Mozambique. Madiba alighted from an army chopper wearing his famous smile and cheerfully greeting all family members and members of the public. Madiba told Mrs Machel, 'Mama, I bought you chocolates.' He called Mazola and me, saying, 'Chaps, can you fetch the chocolates from the chopper.' It was a hot day and Mazola and I went to the chopper. I got in to retrieve the chocolate box while Mazola waited at the foot of the chopper. I passed the box to Mazola and he held it towards his body.

I REMEMBER melted chocolate spilling onto Mazola's torso, and we had to report back to Madiba with chocolates worn as clothes. Can you imagine the embarrassment? Everyone was staring at us as we walked in and Madiba's smile as we walked towards him. The look on Madiba's face was like, 'What the hell?' as well as, 'How can you mess up the gift?' We were clearly the butt of a joke. At least we still had the chocolate box.

Poppy Lukhele

I REMEMBER when we were in transit from point A to B, our whole motorcade crossed over an island while getting onto the freeway. We were on our way from Mahlamba Ndlopfu to Houghton and it was peak-hour traffic. Madiba noticed and asked through the bodyguard Number One who was travelling with him in the main car why we were doing that. He told the bodyguard to tell us how we were breaking the law. We all ignored this. Later we teased among ourselves that he must have got his driver's licence on Robben Island.

I REMEMBER that when Madiba was invited for lunch or dinner he made sure that the host knew that he travelled with a team of twenty people and that he would not eat if the whole team was not offered food.

I REMEMBER when the Virgin Atlantic boss Richard Branson invited him for lunch at his residence in England, he had to accommodate the rest of the team in his garage or else Madiba would not have eaten.

I REMEMBER that Madiba would say 'Darling' when talking to Aunt Gra, and we would, during our debriefing sessions after work tease each other and call each other 'Darling' too.

Anton 'Kallie' Calitz

I REMEMBER during a visit to Maputo, nine-year-old Minette Bruwer handed Madiba a birthday card as he stepped off the SA Air Force Falcon. Later the same day, the Bruwer family's phone rang in Maputo and Minette's mother answered. The caller identified himself as Madiba and said he wished to personally thank the family for the birthday wishes received. Thinking initially it a hoax call, she soon realised it was indeed Madiba.

I REMEMBER when Madiba was travelling to Qunu, Transkei. The flight was scheduled from Waterkloof airforce base to Mthatha, and a last-minute arrangement resulted in an unscheduled stopover at Durban airport. We were informed that Madiba was expecting a brief visit at the airport, before proceeding to Mthatha.

I REMEMBER that as we taxied to a stop at Durban I expected the visitor to come meet Madiba at the aircraft. Unexpectedly Madiba informed us that we would be visiting a patient at the St Augustine's Hospital, 15 kilometres from the airport. We objected immediately because no prior transport arrangements had been made; it was not planned for. I remember Madiba casually replying that he had arranged for a friend to come and collect us. 'She will be here any minute now,' he said nonchalantly. Although this was against security protocol we reluctantly agreed to the plan.

I REMEMBER Madiba's friend arriving shortly after and, after apologising for being late, off we went, Madiba and myself on the back seat, and Mike Maponya in front with Madiba's friend who was driving a normal mid-size sedan. We arranged with Superintendent Deon Botha of the Provincial VIP unit to meet us at St Augustine's with a motorcade, to secure the return trip. The 15-kilometre trip to the hospital was uneventful and I was relieved that we remained undetected.

I REMEMBER the breach in security protocol was addressed shortly thereafter by the protection services management team and Madiba apologised for arranging his 'own' transport.

I REMEMBER Madiba visiting one of his former prison warders and his wife at a retirement home in Pretoria. They enjoyed tea together and the sincerity of the reunion was that of old friends reuniting.

I REMEMBER Madiba had renovations done at his Houghton residence. He wanted to thank the building team and asked me to buy two sheep for them. Slightly confused, I asked if it should be carcasses or live sheep. Madiba responded firmly that it should be live sheep, while handing over a sufficient amount.

I REMEMBER sourcing the sheep on a smallholding east of Silverton the following day, much to the delight of the construction team.

Adrian Sydow

I REMEMBER in 1998 we were in Mauritius for a meeting of SADC and Mr Mandela was in his room in a meeting. We left the hotel to have dinner in the evening and during the meal we received a call from the hotel saying Mr Mandela wanted to see the doctor who was at dinner with us. We finished dinner and rushed back to the hotel. We had to wait outside his room for about two hours because he was having physiotherapy. I went in and asked in my Afrikaans accent if Mr Mandela still wanted to see the doctor. He replied in Afrikaans: 'Nee, ek is nou moeg en gaan nou slaap' [No, I am tired and I'm going to sleep]. The way he changed his language to the person he was speaking to showed how the president had a lot of respect for everyone around him and took no one for granted.

Moeketsi D Matlabe

I REMEMBER we were in Maputo with Madiba. Mum was at her office that day and I had to collect his newspapers at Maputo airport after they were flown in from South Africa every morning. But on this particular day, something was not right. One of the newspapers had an article that said 'Mandela has died'. Now imagine the stress I was going through that I had to be the one to break the news to him. Zelda la Grange called me before the newspapers were collected to warn me of the article. When the newspapers finally arrived, I took them to the house; he was waiting for them. I greeted him and he responded, but I had hidden them behind my back so he could not see them. He realised something was not right and he said, 'You don't seem to be yourself today, what did you do last night?' Still with the papers behind my back I said, 'Tata, I have your papers with me.' He said, 'Where are they? I have been waiting so long to update myself with what is happening in the world.'

I REMEMBER that I took a breath and said, 'Before you read your papers, there is something I have to warn you about,' and he paused and looked at me. I said, 'There is a newspaper that is saying you have died.' Believe you me, that was the hardest thing I ever had to say in my entire life. He looked at me with his right hand covering his wide open mouth and his eyes in disbelief. He said, 'Gee whiz! These people can't wait for me to die, why are they in so much of a hurry that they want me to die? I wonder what they are going to get if I die.' For me that was enough, I just wanted to get out of the room. There it was, on the front page of the *Sowetan* newspaper. I took two steps backwards trying to get out of the room and he said, 'No wait.' He wanted to interrogate me further. Luckily someone knocked at the door and interrupted him. I was called outside before he could say what he wanted to say, I asked permission from him to go and see what was taking place, and he agreed.

I REMEMBER there were people from the SABC who also heard the news about his passing and wanted to prove if it was true or false. I tried to explain to them that Tata just received the same news from me and that he was shocked. They said they wanted to see him even if there was no interview. I consulted my office in Pretoria and Zelda la Grange to inform them of the situation. Fortunately they agreed. I had to go and tell Tata that the people from SABC were there and they wanted an interview with him about the rumour that he had died. He couldn't believe his ears. 'Are these people for real?' he asked me. I said, 'Tata I have no idea what they want from you, but I have spoken to Zeldina and she said you can talk to them but "just be careful what you say".' We laughed. He eventually came out of the house and stood by the door and asked how everyone was, even the SABC staff. They took pictures of him and he said he was fine. Then he went back inside.

I REMEMBER on one of our trips to New York, Madiba was invited to a surprise party for Robert de Niro at his flat. We arrived before de Niro did and when he arrived he was very happy to see Madiba. The real surprise was the arrival of Muhammad Ali. The two of them couldn't get over seeing each other and kept hugging and holding each other's hands like kids. They sat on a couch staring at each other and smiling. Eventually it was time for them to take pictures in a boxing position, looking at each other as if they were in the ring. We all stood behind Madiba to guard against a punch from Ali, but it never came.

I REMEMBER that after the party we went back to the hotel, and there was BeBe Winans, all set to perform for his favourite person. He sang 'Born for this' to Madiba. I had never seen Madiba cry before but BeBe made him cry that day. It was like BeBe was talking to him on a personal level about his life and what God had made him for. As he sang he pointed at Madiba and all I could see was teary eyes. Madiba took out his handkerchief and wiped his eyes. I also got emotional and also had tears in my eyes. After the performance he thanked BeBe for the beautiful song.

I REMEMBER that on the day of our departure Madiba's knees were giving him trouble and he found it difficult to get up the stairs of the aircraft. He paused and I decided to push him from behind with my shoulder, lifting him a little for support. It boosted him and his movement got faster with each step. He just kept on saying, 'Good. Good. Good,' as he took one step at a time, and that was the quickest time he got into the aircraft, he was very impressed.

Achmat Dangor

I REMEMBER going on a trip with Madiba to Australia where a singer called Kylie Minogue had done something for the Nelson Mandela Children's Fund. So in Canberra before he met the prime minister we were taken through the protocol. There were four couples and a young woman standing at the end. The couples were regional ministers with their partners and the prime minister standing in the middle. The protocol officer said, 'Mr Mandela will come here, he will then greet the prime minister who will then step out and the prime minister will introduce him to the others.' So I see this young woman and I ask, 'Now who is she supposed to be?' And she says to me, 'Kylie Minogue.' I warned her, I said, 'Put her in front.' She said, 'We can't do that.' Madiba walked into the room and when he got to where the prime minister steps out and he sees Kylie Minogue. 'Kylie! Kylie!' and he walks right past the prime minister and gives her his hand. 'How are you my girl?' And then he turns around and says, 'Introduce me to all these important people.' The protocol officer behind me was trying to kick me but I had warned them.

I REMEMBER when Madiba met Queen Elizabeth II at Buckingham Palace and apart from asking if he could call her 'Elizabeth', when he saw the woman who was going to serve tea he went to greet her first before he greeted the Queen. But this was just Madiba's nature.

I REMEMBER when he went to Washington DC and met President George W Bush in the White House he did exactly the same thing. He ignored the president and greeted the butler.

I REMEMBER that at the end of 2001 Audrey, my wife, got a job with the United Nations Population Fund that dealt with African youth. She had had to follow me all over, from Scotland to South Africa and then to New York. So I thought it's time that I followed her. So I went to tell him that I am leaving the Children's Fund and I had mentored a successor. He said, 'Oh, so who is this woman leading you by your nose?' And I tried to explain to him, 'Madiba, it's my wife and she's done so much.' 'Yes. Yes. Yes.' Then they had this farewell dinner and when they gave me a gift he got up to present it to me from the stage. He said, 'We want to say farewell to a friend here but I first want to point out the woman who is leading him by his nose.'

I REMEMBER that in 2004 when I was working for UNAIDS we were at the Bangkok Aids conference where Madiba was one of the main speakers, together with Bill Clinton. South Africa's Health Minister Manto Tshabalala-Msimang, who at the time was against the use of ARVS for HIV and promoted natural remedies instead, asked to see Madiba before he made his speech. Before she went in, she looked into the room where Madiba was and said to me, 'You! You are trying to poison Madiba's mind.' She went in and I could see through the window that they were arguing. And Madiba got up; he opened the door and called me: 'Come in here.'

I REMEMBER him telling me, 'This lady says I can't think for myself and you put things into my head. Does she think I'm stupid? I know nothing about anything at all?' She gets up and Madiba says to her, 'Don't go and make a fool of our country.' She bowed to him and said, 'Goodbye'. She went into the exhibition hall and set up her display of natural remedies and left the conference.

I REMEMBER when we were starting the Centre of Memory and Dialogue at the Nelson Mandela Foundation and we had a consultation with people who supported the idea. Madiba called me aside and he said, 'Listen here, when you bring people together in a room who agree with each other, that's a chat. If you want dialogue, bring together people who disagree with each other.' And that is in fact how one of the first big dialogues started, the time when the South African government was not allowing people access to the national archive.

I REMEMBER getting a call from Jakes Gerwel and being told, 'The Old Man wants to speak to you and it's important that you listen very very carefully because you also have to give back to your country.' And then Madiba came on and asked me if I enjoyed my stay at UNAIDS because it's time to come home to fight the HIV battle here. I wanted to say to him, 'But Madiba, you know I've just settled in.' I'd just been there for two years from 2004 and Zachary our son was just born. Madiba was so persuasive that I said, 'Okay, I'll send confirmation to Jakes.' He yelled, 'Jakes! The man says yes!'

Shirley Naidu

I REMEMBER when I attended the job interview with Tata and Mum for the position as their residence manageress, including cooking for them and their family and guests. It was a Sunday after I had worked a shift at The Galley restaurant in Fish Hoek. I was very nervous and anxious and didn't know what to say and how to be.

I REMEMBER that they were both so warm and made me feel so comfortable. Tata asked all the questions and was so kind. I was scared to take the job and tried every excuse for him to not employ me — but he made me feel at ease.

I REMEMBER telling Tata that I would feel bad to leave my employer as they had put food on my plate for the last ten years, especially to leave during the busiest season when I was most needed. Tata said he would wait for me, whenever I was ready and I should be loyal to him too. I felt honoured.

I REMEMBER one morning Tata had a breakfast appointment with Professor Jakes Gerwel but he was delayed. Prof had been waiting for thirty minutes. I knocked at Madiba's bedroom door to let him know that Prof had been waiting for a very long time. Tata asked me, 'Darling, who are you working for here? Me or Prof?'

Then he laughed and made a point of telling Prof I scolded him. After that it became a private joke whenever Prof was around — Tata liked to tease him with it.

I REMEMBER when my daughter's friend's bicycle was stolen from our garden. Madiba overheard the phone call and, the very next day, he visited my home to see how high our wall was. He immediately arranged for sponsorship to have a fence installed. I will always remember his concern and sincere care over everyone's wellbeing. I learnt so much from his humility and his kindness. He always treated you as part of the family.

I REMEMBER whenever I felt down, he always knew something was wrong and he always showed so much love and tried to cheer me up.

Thembeka Mufamadi

I REMEMBER Tata sharing how 'Oom Ray', Raymond Mhlaba, his comrade on Robben Island, helped political prisoners, especially the newcomers, to understand that the African National Congress and the South African Communist Party were two separate organisations. Tata would say that many of these young chaps assumed that Congress and the Party were one and the same thing. Tata told me of this incident as I began to assist him to write his presidential memoirs as a researcher.

I REMEMBER Tata's instruction to put in a request to the government archives for access to Cabinet minutes taken during his term in office for use in his memoirs.

I REMEMBER contacting Mr Frank Chikane, the then State Cabinet Secretary, who explained that Cabinet minutes are classified as top secret state documents that are not accessible to the public which included Tata himself as the former president. Tata accepted this verdict without any hesitation.

Dudu Buthelezi

I REMEMBER when I first started working for Madiba and he asked me to make him a cup of coffee. He said, 'half a cup.' When I took him the coffee he was reading a newspaper and I said, 'Tata, here is your coffee.' He told me, 'I said half a cup.' He just continued reading his newspaper. I didn't know what to do. I went back to the kitchen where I met a colleague. She laughed and told me that it had to be exactly half a cup. I had given him three-quarters of a cup.

I REMEMBER when I went into his office once wearing my spectacles and he said, 'Dudu you look so beautiful.' I said, 'Thank you Tata.' And he said, 'Tell me, do you now have a boyfriend?' I could not answer.

I REMEMBER when the Reverend Malusi Mpumlwana came to visit Madiba. I offered him some coffee but he asked for water. Madiba said he would take coffee. After I brought it to them I went back to the kitchen. After a while the Reverend came to the kitchen to tell me that Madiba wanted to see me. I went in and he said, 'Dudu, please sit down.' When I was sitting he said, 'I would like to thank you for treating my visitors so well.' I was shocked because it was just an honour to me.

I remember when my husband Selby passed on in 2006 and Madiba called me to his office and asked me to sit with him. His words are still so fresh in my mind. 'I know that you are in pain but when I look at you I see a strong woman. You must take it easy; God will heal whatever you are going through. Don't stop doing the right thing.'

Ethel Arends

I REMEMBER that sometimes Madiba would call the staff to his office. We would all go in and one by one we would shake his hand and greet him.

I REMEMBER being in awe of him but he would make you feel relaxed and comfortable in his presence.

I REMEMBER when he was diagnosed with prostate cancer. He called us all together in the office and said: 'The doctors have just told me that I have prostate cancer. Don't be alarmed when you read about it in the newspapers. I will be fine, I am okay.'

I REMEMBER when my mother passed away; Madiba came to our flat in Eldorado Park and paid his respects to the family. It meant a lot to my family and me.

Lydia Bergström

I REMEMBER Mr Mandela as the consummate gentleman. He was full of genuine warmth and had a consistently gracious aura about him. What I remember most, however, is his remarkable ability to sense and to alleviate other people's discomfort.

I REMEMBER quite well the first time I met Madiba – I had prepared for the moment by reading up on Xhosa culture. Traditionally when meeting a leader, one should not look them in the eye, to respectfully show one is of a lower distinction. When I entered his office, I was determined to show Mr Mandela respect and so I looked down. After a short pause, I saw his hand stretched out to shake mine. I quickly looked up and saw the corner of his mouth tighten into a bemused smile. He shook my hand and thanked me for being on board the team, telling me to 'Hold the fort, Lydia,' as he departed for his first international trip after resigning from the Presidency. I never once called Mr Mandela, Madiba. For me, he was always 'Sir'.

I REMEMBER that Mr Mandela used to receive many gifts, every single month, and among them came artwork. Hundreds of pieces would arrive, from large paintings by famous artists to simpler drawings from children. One day a large and exquisitely rendered piece arrived from a well-known artist, who due to a birth defect could not use her hands and painted with a brush in her mouth. Madiba was so moved by her portrait that he invited her to tea, in order to thank her personally. The morning of her arrival, a colleague and myself went in to serve the tea, when my colleague blanked, not knowing where to place the teacup. Madiba quickly stepped in, asking gently, 'How do you take your tea?' and the problem was fixed.

I REMEMBER that, many times, Madiba would ask us staff members simple questions like, 'Lydia, have you eaten?' His concern was boundless. If he suspected we were being polite, he would begin to inquire in more detail — a smile always present in his voice.

I REMEMBER on a flight with Madiba back from Qunu, the airplane hit tremendous turbulence. I was a nervous flyer and tried to keep a stoic face. I looked over at Madiba. He had his feet up on a chair, looking up over his newspaper at me, totally relaxed with a slight smile on his face. He exuded an atmosphere of reassurance without saying a word.

I REMEMBER that Madiba had extremely good manners; he was never derogatory and never snide. The way he spoke was always perfect — he was a natural orator. He spoke beautifully; his English was exceptional, as well as his isiXhosa, isiZulu and Afrikaans among others.

I REMEMBER that Mr Mandela also had a gentle sense of humour — he asked me once to contact a Cabinet minister, asking if he could arrive at the office quite early the next day. I inquired if perhaps another time would suit Madiba should the minister be occupied, but he merely smiled at me and chuckled, 'Oh, he'll be there.'

I REMEMBER that Madiba was the embodiment of selflessness. Whenever he spoke to anyone, anyone at all — the cleaners, a staff member, a gardener, royalty, ambassadors — he would speak to them as if they were the most important person in the world at that time.

I REMEMBER that Madiba's office would constantly receive requests for photographs, autographs, books to be signed, and invitations to hundreds of events every month. We kept the barrage in order, however sometimes people managed to sneak through — diplomats and ambassadors were the worst, asking such favours of him directly. Very often, Madiba would turn to one of us and note, 'Well, you'll have to take that up with my boss, I'm afraid.' One afternoon he was signing books, and after what seemed like the hundredth book I asked him if he ever grew tired or irritated at the volume. He paused, looked up at me, and said, 'One gets used to it. It is what is expected, and what we must do.' That is Madiba — the epitome of grace.

Bridgette Prince

I REMEMBER how Madiba taught me to fight for a cause that I believe in, to take responsibility for the outcome and always to support those who need us.

I REMEMBER when I joined the Nelson Mandela Foundation in 2000; Madiba requested that we explore the result and impact of anti-retroviral drugs on HIV-infected patients. This led to the NMF setting up pilot sites in Lusikisiki, in the Transkei, at the GF Jooste Hospital in Cape Town and through the Tshepang Trust. Our data showed that we could contribute to extending the lives of those living with HIV/AIDS.

I REMEMBER that Madiba taught me that any intervention or programme must be based on evidence and this saw the Nelson Mandela Foundation lead on one of the largest HIV household surveys on the African continent. The information gathered ensured that we were able to make informed decisions and the evidence had a fundamental impact on policy not only in South Africa but in the world. All of these efforts demanded that we think selflessly of a disease which at the time was ravaging our people but not receiving the kind of attention it required.

Vimla Naidoo & Sahm Venter

I REMEMBER how Madiba showed through his leadership that by taking the lead anything is possible, even in the face of adversity. He taught me that this is what leadership means, leaders must lead.

Buyi Sishuba

I REMEMBER in 2001 when Madiba came to join his staff at our end-of-year Christmas party in the garden of his house. He started reminiscing with us and telling his usual anecdotes. The one thing that stood out for me was when he said that he liked to tell people that in life you must always strive to be in the back, in that way no one notices you and you are able to manoeuvre without anyone being aware.

I REMEMBER that he told us when you are in the front, people see you and it is easy for them to pull you down and destroy you before you even reach your destination. That really hit home and I try to apply it in my life.

Boniswa Nyati

I REMEMBER the first encounter I had with Mr Mandela when he said, 'When I am dead and knock at heaven's door they will ask, "Who is that?" And I will say, "I am Nelson Mandela", and they will say, "Try next door, there is no ANC here".'

I REMEMBER when Mr Mandela and Mrs Machel would come to view the gifts and awards they had been sent from around the world. I showed him a comb and he said, 'I would love to have this comb, maybe the person who sent it had the intention of changing the colour of my hair from grey to black.'

I REMEMBER that the Resource Centre which I ran was established from the tonnes of books sent to Mr Mandela from across the world. He would often pick books himself from the collection and I would personally deliver them to his residence.

I REMEMBER when one morning he requested us to get him three Afrikaans books, which we did and he commented, 'One must be able to read and write all South African languages, if you want to communicate effectively with people.'

I REMEMBER after I took some Americans, who I had been volunteering with at a Pretoria home for Mandela Day, to see Mr Mandela's house. Fortunately for us, he saw us passing by and called us in. I had to introduce everyone and tell him what we had done for the day. He was very excited to hear about our Mandela Day work and thanked the visitors.

I REMEMBER on 5 August 2008 when we celebrated his 90th birthday with him. We sang 'Happy birthday' to him and gave him a cake and gifts bought by the Nelson Mandela Foundation staff. One was a huge, soft white blanket. I wrapped him and Mrs Machel in it and whispered to them, 'With this blanket your love for each other will always be warm.'

I REMEMBER when he came to the office on 24 November 2009 to present us with long-service certificates in recognition of our service to the Foundation and his work to reach out to communities.

Denise Abrahams

I REMEMBER when I was in excruciating pain at the office, I told Zelda and she referred me to her doctor. After consulting with her I was told that my appendix was about to burst and that I needed emergency surgery. I went to a private clinic where they then removed my appendix. The care was really bad, as it took a couple hours for them to just bring me ice. The next day I heard a commotion in the corridor and saw everyone outside rushing around in a panic. I didn't know what was happening and thought that somebody may have passed away.

I REMEMBER seeing one of Madiba's bodyguards poking his head into my room and then knew what was happening. The next moment Madiba was in my ward. He spoke to the doctor about my surgery and how I was recovering. He sat by my bedside, surrounded by his protectors and asked me to lift my gown to show him where I was cut. 'Tata, there is no way I'm picking up my clothes to show you with your men in the room,' I said with a smile on my face.

I REMEMBER all the other patients, hospital visitors and staff peeking into my room for the rest of my stay to see who this mysterious person was that Madiba came to see. Needless to say, the service at the hospital improved dramatically. That day I recognised the true meaning of greatness — as a man of his stature, he took the time out of his very busy schedule just to see me, his PA who only had a simple appendectomy. Such was Tata's character, that he never looked up or down at anyone. It didn't matter whether you were a security guard or a president, Madiba always made you feel special. My Madiba, my hero!

Lwaephe Selepe

I REMEMBER as a young man I always wished to meet Mr Nelson Mandela and the first time I was introduced to him, I was very excited and shaking. After the meet and greet I didn't shake anyone else's hand.

I REMEMBER when Mama Graça left on official duties, medics slept at the house like the protectors did. When we slept, Tata would come in our room and check on us. When we realised he was there, we would say, 'Tata, why? You must sleep.' He would say, 'You are my child as well, I must check on you.' Then he would go back to bed.

I REMEMBER in 2008 I was in his lounge shortly after Beyoncé and Jay-Z visited Tata, he called me and said, 'Where's the medic?' 'I'm the medic, Tata.' 'Oh, you'll forgive me, I'm very old.' And then Tata went and sat on his sofa and he asked me, 'Are you married?' I said, 'No Tata, I'm not married.' He said, 'I've got a young lady who is doing a very good job for me and I want you to meet her. And after you meet her, I'm going to buy you a car and a house.' Ay, I was excited! Then Tata picked up the phone, 'Meme, I want you to come here.' I wasn't in Meme's good books, but you can't say, 'No, Tata.' Meme came and Tata broke the news to her, 'This young man has been doing a good job for me for a long time.

I want you, Meme, to tell my grandson to take you to a restaurant somewhere. I want you to talk, I told him what to say. You are not married, Meme?' 'No, I am not married, Tata.' And we started staring at one another, we were not so friendly with one another. We went out and I told Meme, 'Meme, you know I can't marry you.' We didn't go back to Tata and tell him that we are actually not on good terms.

I REMEMBER one day we were sitting at the house and he decided to go to the CNA in Killarney to look for a book. As we entered the mall, the place turned into a mess. Everybody left their posts to go running for Madiba. He would go like, 'Oh, how are you?' I don't think he got a book. He just wanted to be among people that day.

I REMEMBER thinking that working with a statesman you would expect to be treated like a servant, but in his house, Madiba was really treating us like his own children. He even once called me 'Son of the house'.

Joe Ditabo

I REMEMBER that Madiba used to call me, 'Young man Joe'.

I REMEMBER that if there was one thing that would make Madiba angry, it was if someone did not respect time.

I REMEMBER one day when I was in the convoy driving him to Gallagher Estate to address a Cosatu conference. He arrived fifteen minutes before it was due to start but the Cosatu leaders were not there. Madiba told his driver if the leaders had not arrived in ten minutes he was going to leave. We were driving towards the exit when the leaders arrived. They stopped their cars in front of our convoy so that we couldn't leave. They got out of their cars and begged Madiba to stay. Madiba was angry but he told his driver to take him back to the hall. The conference started and Madiba was introduced. He got onto the stage and just stood there for five minutes without saying a single word. Not even a smile.

I REMEMBER that the audience was shocked so a Cosatu leader led them in political slogans. Then they stopped to give Madiba a chance to speak but he just stood there. The leader got the crowd to shout more slogans. Madiba started his speech. He said what he had to say and then he just left the stage and went straight to his car.

I REMEMBER the Cosatu leader telling the people that unfortunately he could not stay for dinner as he had other plans. But he did not have any other appointment.

Florence Garishe

I REMEMBER one morning in early 2002 when I came to the office and found Madiba sitting behind my reception desk, there were cameras all over. I didn't know what to do, he was busy on the phone talking to someone – just like a real receptionist – so I just sat on the couch. After finishing the call he apologised for taking my work space. I smiled and said, 'Thank you, Tata.'

I REMEMBER receiving a phone call, the voice sounded like Madiba's but I was unsure if that was a prank or not. I thought Madiba would have called Zelda straight to her direct number or mobile not via the board. I heard his voice saying, 'Good morning, I am sorry to disturb you, can you please put me through to Zelda?' I told him to hold on for Zelda. I started panicking when I found out that Zelda was busy on her line, I didn't know whether I should run to her or call someone nearby to her to tell her that Madiba was on the line. I just decided to go back to him and tell him that Zelda was busy on the phone and enquired if I may tell her to return his call when she was through. He agreed, thanked me for that and said, 'Good bye.'

Meme Kgagara

I REMEMBER a few months after I started working for Madiba and Mum in 2002 I was serving him lunch and I also served him the sweet wine that he liked. He asked me, 'Do you take any wine?' I said, 'No, Tata I don't.' He said, 'But you should taste this one.' I said, 'No, Tata I am not sure. I am not taking any but there is this sparkling wine that we take when we have special occasions.' And he said, 'No, you must go and get dry wine, it's good for the heart.'

I REMEMBER that he said, 'By the way, I know you are from Hammanskraal, so I am not saying you should go and buy the whole bottle, sit under a tree and drink the whole thing. Only one glass with your meal.' I think that because he is the one who said it, I started thinking that it's a good thing to take wine with my meals. That's when I started to take one glass of dry red wine, cabernet sauvignon with my food.

I REMEMBER that he once said, 'Come here young lady.' So we sat down and he said to me, 'How many boyfriends do you have?' I said, 'Oh Tata, I only have one.' 'No, no, no, no, no, no. I'm asking you how many boyfriends do you have?' We were stuck on that topic for a few minutes. He wanted me to say a number, but I said 'it's one'. He said, 'No, no. You've got to have three or four, a young attractive woman like you. No, no, surely you do have more.' I said, 'But, Tata, I don't.'

I REMEMBER that I was sort of detained by him and Mum came down the stairs. Then he said to me, 'We are still going to finish this discussion. You can go now.' I was like, 'Oh my goodness.'

I REMEMBER that there was a time when his eyes were tired of reading newspapers and he would ask me to read to him from all the newspapers including the Afrikaans ones. When I read from *Beeld* to him he would make me read so loudly that it felt like I was doing recitation.

I REMEMBER that every day when I met Tata he would first ask me how I am and then he would ask about my children and my extended family. Tata did not treat us like his workers but as his family and his children.

Makano Morojele

I REMEMBER hearing the shuffling of feet down the passage of Mr Mandela's home at Shambala in the Waterberg, towards the dining room where we awaited his entrance. He and Mrs Machel were speaking so loudly I could hear every word! They were talking about getting a builder in to fix a crack in the wall and Madiba wondering if a black-owned construction firm had built the house.

I REMEMBER thinking, am I really going to have dinner with Mr Mandela, and how did that come about? I hoped to be able to respond intelligently to his questions yet at the same time I hoped he wouldn't ask me any questions lest I embarrass myself by giving responses not befitting his stature.

I REMEMBER that as he walked into the dining room, our eyes locked for a moment, and immediately I saw my father's eyes. Memories came flooding back of how my father used to look at me with reassuring eyes that saw deep into my soul. During dinner he enthralled us all with graphic details of how he was circumcised at the age of sixteen at the traditional initiation school.

I REMEMBER then feeling as I used to feel when my father would tell stories of himself as a young boy looking after sheep in the mountains of Lesotho. I truly felt the presence of my father telling us ordinary stories about his ordinary life.

Elaine McKay

I REMEMBER Sir Richard Branson brought Brad Pitt to meet Madiba to explain the work they were doing to eliminate landmines on the African continent. When Brad was introduced to Madiba, Madiba asked him what he did for a living. He told Madiba he was an actor and asked if Madiba had seen any of his films. Madiba simply said 'no'.

I REMEMBER when Madiba agreed to a staff Christmas party with our children. A photo opportunity was arranged, and my son who was two at the time got on Madiba's lap and said: 'I love you Mr Mandela.' One of our German consultants, Heiko, ushered in his daughter, also about two, to Madiba and she was clearly not interested in sitting on his lap. Heiko tried to encourage her, and Mandela said: 'Leave her; she's from the old South Africa.'

I REMEMBER when Will Smith was asked to launch MTV Base Africa, and he made arrangements to meet Madiba during the visit. Ludacris, who was also on the line-up, desperately wanted to meet Madiba too. He arrived for the meeting with his entourage, one of whom made a point of telling Madiba that he recently acquired a piece of Madiba's 'art' – the much disputed fundraising attempt based on Madiba's hand prints. Madiba was quietly seething and did not smile until they left.

I REMEMBER a few weeks before I gave birth to my daughter, we scheduled a 46664 event at the international AIDS conference in Bangkok and I was told by British Airways at the last minute that they would not allow me to fly because I was too close to my due date. On his return from Bangkok, Madiba asked me why I wasn't there. I explained and he said I could have come on the Anglo jet with him.

I REMEMBER laughing when he said he would have helped me deliver, if the baby arrived early. He said that in his day, women would come in from the fields, deliver their babies and go back to work. I responded that maternal deaths during childbirth were probably high 'in his day'. He laughed and sighed, then added, 'You are probably right.'

I REMEMBER being delighted that he expressed a willingness to deliver my daughter himself. She ended up arriving four weeks early and was almost born in our office.

Yase Godlo

I REMEMBER when I worked in the finance department of the Nelson Mandela Foundation and I had to take documents to Madiba's house. I entered through the kitchen and his staff said he was having lunch and I should, 'Go and talk to him, just at least go and say hi.' I went into the dining room and I said, 'Hello Mr Mandela. My name is Yase and I'm from the Foundation, I have been sent to give you these documents.' Immediately he invited me to sit and have lunch and then started interrogating me about where I am from and if I knew the Godlo family from East London. I told him no, that I was from Qanda and the parts that are closer to Mthatha. He told me that I was part of the Xhamela clan, like Walter Sisulu.

I REMEMBER him speaking with me in English and then mixing it up with isiXhosa. I could talk to him like I would have spoken to an uncle or an old man from the community who I have just met. I didn't eat lunch with him, I felt intimidated. I mean this was Madiba and he was inviting me to sit. I sat for a bit but I told them to not serve me food. Fortunately, Meme came in and made an excuse for me to go back to the office and I left.

I REMEMBER another day some important person was visiting Madiba's house and we were asked to go there. But before it started Madiba was having a full-on conversation with his grandchildren. I came into the room but they couldn't see me. Madiba was asking them what they were doing at school; what were they going to do next and scolding some of them saying, 'I hear you've not been doing well in school, what is happening?'

I REMEMBER that I could not help but see Madiba at that moment not as an icon, some sort of celebrity or this supernatural person — he was just someone's grandfather. The children were explaining themselves and you could see that they were very uncomfortable. But it was also a happy moment because while he was holding them to account the conversation was more about their self-development.

I REMEMBER when we had the Nelson Mandela Annual Lecture in Kliptown, Soweto and we had created a special ramp for Mr Mandela to access the hall from the entrance. We had this choir Imilonji kaNtu, which was going to perform that day. The choir was backstage when Madiba came in. Even though he came early we were worried about the schedule of the event because he stopped and chatted with everyone and people took pictures with him.

I REMEMBER that every time I experienced him interacting with people I noticed he would give a person cleaning the same level of respect he would give to the president of another country. He would take time and speak to that person with a serious and true interest about who they are. It showed me the human in him and how natural it was for him to acknowledge and respect people.

Verne Harris

I REMEMBER when a foreign politician came to see Madiba, supposedly on a courtesy call. Our team discovered that he had planned to get Madiba's blessing for his election campaign back home. The politician refused to go in when he was asked to sign a confidentiality agreement and sent in two colleagues instead. Madiba was warned. He asked them about their flight to South Africa, the pilots on their plane, what rest they were able to take, the refuelling of the aircraft and when they would return home. When they finally asked Madiba to bless the election campaign he said, 'No' and added that he would be 'severely criticised' if he did so. Madiba then ended the meeting with more small talk about their departure from South Africa.

I REMEMBER when I had to escort Madiba down the long passage from his office to the front entrance of our office, where there was to be a photo opportunity. He was heavy on my arm by the time we reached my boss, Achmat Dangor, at the entrance, waiting to take Madiba out. 'Ah Achmat,' Madiba said to him, 'now you can do some real work!'

I REMEMBER a day, a December day, when Madiba called all the staff into his office to thank them for their service during the year. 'This might be the last time,' he said, 'because I am ancient now. You know, when I get to the pearly gates, they will ask me "who are you?" I will say "Madiba!" They will respond: "Where do you come from?" I will say "South Africa!" "Ah," they will say, "you are that Madiba. No, you have come to the wrong gates. You see those ones far away down there, the very warm ones? Those are your gates."' He paused, before the punch line: 'But don't worry. Big business and the ANC will be there to assist me.' And then, of course, the vintage Madiba laugh.

I REMEMBER when our sessions discussing archives and narratives of the past had become a burden to him. On the last time, several of us put such questions to him for a particular project he became clearly irritated and said: 'Listen chaps, at my age you remember certain things and not others. I'm afraid I don't remember any of the things you've raised. Now, would you mind if I get back to my newspapers?'

Anthea Josias

I REMEMBER visiting Madiba at his home in Houghton in 2006. I was there to greet him before taking up further studies in the US less than a month later. The house was quiet and Tata was reading the newspaper in a very large living room. It seemed as if something in the newspaper that day made him cross, and he complained about somebody he was reading about who needed to consult more. Madiba then went on to talk about the importance of being part of a collective, and its embeddedness in the cultures of the liberation movement. He spoke about drawing on the insights of the collective to influence our actions, telling a story of his own relationship with Tata Walter Sisulu and others on Robben Island.

I REMEMBER the conversation was short but it was an important one. It is still a reminder to me to recognise and steer away from selfish individualism, both in myself and others. It was also an affirmation of my beliefs, at the time about going out into a world where those same values were not always held in the same regard.

Oupa Ngwenya

I REMEMBER that while the powerful and the well-endowed sought his company, Madiba's love for children claimed the dearest place in his heart. Every year he celebrated his birthday with them.

I REMEMBER the thrill as his motorcade arrived at number 21 Eastwold Way for the Nelson Mandela Children's Fund annual celebration.

I REMEMBER how parents would obstruct the view of young ones as they surged forward from their designated seats just to be in a picture with Madiba. The children would be seated and orderly waiting their turn to sing, dance, recite poems, read messages, and to savour the meet and greet opportunity with the 'birthday boy'.

I REMEMBER one parent bolting to the front to the red chair in which Madiba was seated. With a child in one arm and the other holding a mobile phone, she was, in a split-second, sitting on Madiba's lap while taking a picture of herself, the child and Madiba.

I REMEMBER that Madiba smiled understandingly through the episode and his security politely ushered the mother and child back to their seats.

I REMEMBER that, in 2005, word got out that the eighty-seven-year-old Madiba was attending the annual general meeting of the Nelson Mandela Children's Fund in Western Jabavu, Soweto. On his departure, the streets were filled with people forming a guard of honour for the passage of his motorcade.

I REMEMBER that his car stopped and Madiba stepped out, waving in acknowledgement of the throngs. There was a forest of clenched black power salutes, ululations and shouts of 'amandla' as his car drove past.

I REMEMBER that Madiba never missed asking after one's health and the welfare of one's next of kin.

I REMEMBER Madiba spotting the big tummy of one of his bodyguards and saying that he must have been well looked after by his spouse. But, he hastened to add, 'ubhasobh' umkhaba'. Loosely translated it meant 'beware of the tummy'. Madiba apparently dreaded having a big tummy.

I REMEMBER when Madiba announced on 1 June 2004 that he was retiring from public life. He said, 'When I told one of my advisors a few months ago that I wanted to retire he growled at me: "You are retired." If that is really the case then I should say I now announce that I am retiring from retirement. I do not intend to hide away totally from the public, but henceforth I want to be in the position of calling you to ask whether I would be welcome, rather than being called upon to do things and participate in events. The appeal therefore is: Don't call me, I'll call you.' The laughter, applause and standing ovation was spontaneous. The media conference did not end without a parting shot: 'Thank you very much for your attention and thank you for being kind to an old man — allowing him to take a rest, even if many of you may feel that after loafing somewhere on an island and other places for twenty-seven years the rest is not really deserved. I thank you.'

I REMEMBER the Children's Fund financial manager Leona Sequeira seeing Madiba and his entourage leaving the premises. He greeted the security guard who was holding the boom for them to go past. Madiba asked him, 'Do you still remember me?' The security guard found it so amusing that Madiba could ask such a question when it should have been other way round.

I REMEMBER the Children's Celebration at the French School in Johannesburg to mark Madiba's 90th birthday. The children came near to listen to his message which was: 'It is ordinary people — men and women, boys and girls — that make the world a special place.' He spoke of his desire to, 'make the society more familiar with the smiles of children rather than their tears'. He added: 'If this were true in our society, our youth would be happier, our families stronger, our communities safer and our government reasonably at peace with its citizens.'

Sunée Rautenbach

I REMEMBER while he was having tea one afternoon and speaking to his household staff, he called me closer and, in not such a soft voice, commented on what a lucky man my father was because I had such an African build and he would be able to get a lot of lobola cattle for me. Who knew my pear shape was valued in another culture?

I REMEMBER how forgiving Madiba was. For the life of me, as the human resources officer of the Nelson Mandela Foundation, I could not dismiss any of his household staff in the six years I worked for him. Oh, I tried, but a couple of days later they were forgiven and back in his employ. He taught me a lot about forgiveness, not so much about HR but, wow, was he a forgiving man.

I REMEMBER when he caught Zelda and I smoking on the stoep outside his office one day and gave us a talking to about the health implications and how he never smoked in his life.

I REMEMBER when Verne presented him with a photo showing him sitting with a group of men with a cigarette in his hand. He had the nerve to say it was just a prop for the photo; that he was just trying to look cool.

I Remember Nelson Mandela

I REMEMBER that no matter where you were in the building you could immediately feel his presence, suddenly there was a more respectful, humble, exciting vibe in the building and it was so contagious.

Shadrack Katuu

I REMEMBER meeting Madiba for the first time in November 2005 a few months after I had started working at the Nelson Mandela Foundation. Verne Harris asked me if I would like to meet him briefly while he was preparing to do a video interview. I told him my name and that I came from Kenya and he told me that he had met President Daniel arap Moi and that they had 'a very nice time' together and 'had some very good chats talking about the past'.

I REMEMBER meeting Madiba for the last time and he asked how Kenya was doing. I assured him that it was recovering from post-election trauma. He said, 'That is good. It is very important for Kenya to do well.' He said, 'In prison we drew a lot of inspiration from the experience of all your freedom fighters.' He asked after Jomo Kenyatta's family and remembered that his daughter, Margaret Kenyatta, served as Nairobi's mayor in the seventies. He asked about Uhuru Kenyatta and said he wanted to meet him.

I REMEMBER almost three months later, on 20 March 2009, Deputy Prime Minister Uhuru Kenyatta met Madiba after speaking at a conference hosted by the NMF.

Shaun Johnson

I REMEMBER the years when I had the priceless privilege of taking our newly selected Mandela Rhodes scholars to meet their patron, Madiba.

I REMEMBER that Madiba always used to say something funny to them first, then something serious.

I REMEMBER young Elias Phaahla asking him: 'How is old age treating you?'

I REMEMBER him replying: 'No, no … just ask me – how am I treating old age?'

I REMEMBER him saying to Godfrey Nzimande: 'As long as you value education you will be a leader.'

I REMEMBER him saying to Obedient Tshabalala: 'You must stress that education now is the qualification for leadership.'

I REMEMBER him telling Kim Smith: 'It was only when I was in jail that I made progress in my studies. Fortunately, you don't have to go through that.'

I REMEMBER Suntosh Pillay asking him, in 2008: 'What is your dream for this country?'

I remember Madiba answering in a flash: 'My dream? My dream has started already — here you are!'

Julia Brown

I REMEMBER the first time I met Madiba was in 2006, at his home in Bishopscourt with my husband and eldest daughter, who was three at the time. Rebekah was painfully shy and refused to even look at him, never mind sit on his lap as he had invited her to do. So funny!

I REMEMBER the last time I had the privilege of meeting Madiba, in 2009, at Shaun Johnson's home in Llandudno. We had arranged an end-of-year luncheon for the Class of 2009 Scholars and Mr Mandela was the guest of honour. As I passed him, after our staff pic with him, he grabbed my hand and asked me how I was. That was a very special moment for me as I really didn't think he knew who I was.

Lee Davies

I REMEMBER going up to Madiba's house to go and assist Meme with a technical issue. As I walked in, Meme grabbed me by the arm and dragged me through to see Madiba. Madiba was sitting alone at his dinner table, just finishing up his meal. Meme proceeded to tell him that she had now traded in black men for white men and there I was, no comment, just a mouthful of teeth. Madiba just laughed, as only he can.

Neo Lekgotla laga Ramoupi

I REMEMBER that on 3 October 2006 I finally came face to face with history, when I met Nelson Mandela – also known as Madiba or 'father of the nation'. For that first meeting, as I am a Motswana, I was wearing my Seshweshwe, a Batswana traditional shirt, like his famous Madiba shirt, with a beaded Xhosa necklace. I felt that was a dignified way for me to show my gratitude for what he means to African people.

I REMEMBER being introduced to him in this way, 'This is Neo Ramoupi, he is completing his PhD about Robben Island!' Madiba immediately said to me, 'Ahh! Which period are you looking at!?' I told him, 'From 1960 to 1991,' and very quickly, Mandela said, 'Thirty-one years, that is very good! I am very impressed!'

I REMEMBER how seriously Mandela went on to 'lecture' us (Dr Mothomang Diaho and myself who were meeting him that day as new staff members) about the importance of acquiring an education for the leadership of our country. Madiba wanted us to believe that the struggle is not over once we complete our doctoral degrees or become medical doctors.

I REMEMBER that the ten to fifteen minutes we spent with Mandela were so intimate that to take out my camera would have disturbed the conversation and the moment. As a result, I do not have a photo with Madiba, and I honestly do not regret it, because I hold those few minutes with Mandela in my mind so clearly it is like it was only yesterday.

Naomi Warren

I REMEMBER the first time Madiba was going to come into the office while I was in the building. The curtains to his office were opened and I was very giddy at the thought that he was coming in. I started working at the Nelson Mandela Foundation in Madiba's real retirement years and he only came into the office on very special occasions. I didn't get much work done while the curtains were open that day as I tried to catch a glimpse of the man himself. All I saw was movement in his office but couldn't make out if it was him or not.

I REMEMBER the first time I saw Madiba in the flesh. It was at a press conference calling for funds for Umkhonto weSizwe veterans. He came into the auditorium assisted and I remember thinking how much he reminded me of my granddad and how old and fragile he was and how it felt like he was looking only at me. His eyes, and the generosity and understanding they reflected, were like that of an elephant – so empathetic but at the same time full of sorrow and remembrance. I cried.

I REMEMBER a few weeks later being told that new staff would be introduced to him that day. We all went up to his office where he sat behind his desk. I think I was third or fourth in line. I do not remember the exact moment of my introduction but I hope I smiled enough for him to know that every ounce of me was grateful for his sacrifices. I hope my handshake was strong enough for him to know what an honour it was to be involved in one of his foundations and continuing his legacy and I hope my eyes expressed my humble joy of being in his presence.

Yoga Coopoo

I REMEMBER admiring how serious Tata was about exercise during our muscle-strengthening sessions. He was aware of what was healthy and what was not, and he enthusiastically tackled any form of training. Tata's vigour was evident in many training sessions. When asked if he could manage another set of exercises, he would never decline and always responded with a concerted and determined, 'Yes, yes.'

I REMEMBER that after working with Tata for a few months, I asked him if I could bring my children to meet him. He agreed, and my two children, Kevanya and Verushen, nineteen and eleven years old respectively at the time, accompanied me. At the time, my son could not effectively pronounce the 'r' sound. 'What is your name?' asked Tata with a smile to my son. 'Verushen,' said my son. However, it sounded like 'Velushen'. 'Ah, Velushen!' greeted Tata warmly. My son, though, felt the pressing need to correct Tata, and quickly retorted, 'No, Verushen'. 'Ah, Velushen!' said Tata again, to which my son replied, 'No, Verushen!' At that point, my intensely embarrassed daughter intervened and stopped my son from correcting Tata any further. Later, my daughter said, 'That's Dr Nelson Mandela! It doesn't matter if he calls you Peter – you let him call you Peter!'

I REMEMBER when I had the privilege of accompanying Tata to Mozambique about three times to continue his exercise regime. One morning during breakfast, I met one of Mama Graça's sons. I remarked he was lucky to be in Tata's midst and to receive Tata's wisdom. Tata replied wittily, 'There was no better teacher than Samora Machel!'

I REMEMBER when I arranged to get an arm ergometer, an upper body machine to help increase Tata's upper body capacity. A health and fitness company was consulted and the machine was duly sent to Tata's home. When Tata saw the equipment, we told him where it was from and its intended purpose, he refused to use it. He said that he has never accepted gifts his whole life, so why should he start now. The machine was promptly returned to the company.

Mothomang Diaho

I REMEMBER when I met Madiba for the first time as a member of his staff at the Nelson Mandela Foundation. He walked in to his office with his trusted personal assistant Zelda la Grange, who introduced me as 'Dr Diaho'.

I REMEMBER that Tata Madiba said to me, 'I have a pain in my heart, can you help me, Doctor?' It came out as a joke, but that never left me because throughout Mandela's life, how can he not have a pain in his heart?

I REMEMBER that famous sense of humour.

I REMEMBER that after the formal introductions, Madiba suddenly became serious and proceeded to lecture us about the importance of education.

Pam Barron

I REMEMBER staying in the background when my colleagues had their pictures taken with Madiba. I will always regret not having an individual picture taken with him.

I REMEMBER when Zelda told him that my brother was the minister of finance.

I REMEMBER when he replied that, 'I chose well'.

I REMEMBER him laughing when I told him, 'He is lucky to have me as a sister.'

Sello Hatang

I REMEMBER when I was taken to meet Madiba for the first time. I had just started work at the Nelson Mandela Foundation and I was taken up to his office. He asked me where I came from and I said the North-West Province. When he asked me which part I said Khuma, near Klerksdorp. He said, 'I remember going to your township and I may even have seen you there.' That was my day made. Not only did he know my township but he may even have spotted me there. When I came out of the meeting I immediately told my colleagues Verne Harris and Shadrack Katuu what Madiba had said to me. They just laughed and told me he says that to everyone. Well for as long as it lasted, Madiba had made me feel very important, like I was *the* guy.

I REMEMBER that Madiba always made everyone in the room feel like they were super important; that they were as important as Nelson Mandela.

I REMEMBER that when people came to see Madiba in his office he would get up, stretch out his hand to them and say, 'My name is Nelson Mandela and you are?' Most of the time his guests were unable to utter a single word in reply. They were in shock.

I REMEMBER the one and only photograph I have with just Madiba and I, taken by Debbie Yazbek. I had walked in with Madiba for an event, he sat down and I started by telling a joke. Madiba laughed so hard, for so long that the whole auditorium erupted in laughter.

Valene Peacock

I REMEMBER the first day I started working with Tata, I was introduced to him by Mr Selepe. He said, 'Tata this is one of our new medics.' He says, 'Oh, okay. What's your name?' So I said, 'I am Valene Peacock.' He said, 'Come again?' When he heard my surname was Peacock he couldn't stop laughing.

I REMEMBER in that first week I asked if I could have a picture with him and when I came in he says, 'Why, with such an old man like me?' He did so much for our country but it didn't go to his head, he remained humble throughout.

I REMEMBER we went to Milpark Hospital to visit someone. We were standing in the elevator. And I was holding a bottle of Perrier water for him. He asked, 'Who's that water for?' I said, 'It's for you in case you get thirsty, Tata'. He said, 'I hope you have some whisky with that water.'

I REMEMBER how Tata never used to like men with big tummies, because he used to be a fit man. So when he saw someone with a big tummy he would call him and say, 'Can I see you in private?' So one day we were at the Nelson Mandela Foundation and he asked me to call one of the protectors who he had been looking at the whole time. I went to call him and he said, 'I want to see you in private.' He said, 'Yes Tata, I'm coming.' He went into Tata's office, they closed the door and then he came out laughing. So I asked him, 'What did he tell you?' He said, 'No, I must do something about my stomach. It's too big.'

I REMEMBER he used to call us and say, 'I'm in the mood to speak Afrikaans now. Come and sit here.' And he would speak Afrikaans and then he would laugh at people who didn't understand and say, 'Hulle verstaan nie wat ons nou se, nê?' [They don't understand what we are saying.]

I REMEMBER one of my proudest moments was accompanying him to President Jacob Zuma's first inauguration. He was very happy to be there.

Kerileng Marumo

I REMEMBER when I first met Madiba in person in 2009. I couldn't believe my eyes. I thought I was dreaming. He asked me my name, surname and where I come from. I was not so sure which name to give him since I have two names and the first is difficult to pronounce. To my surprise he pronounced it so well and said 'Kerileng!' with a Xhosa accent. He asked me, 'That is a Setswana name, right?' I said, 'Yes!' with big smile. He was holding my hands so tight and his hands were so soft like a baby's.

Lucia Raadschelders

I REMEMBER the first time I 'met' Madiba was when I was working underground for the ANC. He managed to send us coded messages from Victor Verster Prison.

I REMEMBER when I was working at the ANC headquarters in 1994 I would bump into Madiba in the lift. The first time I was terribly excited to finally meet THE MAN! Coming from the Anti-Apartheid Movement and the ANC underground he had been elevated to a very special platform in my eyes.

I REMEMBER that when we were in the lift together he would politely say, 'hello' and smile.

Njabulo S Ndebele

I REMEMBER my wife, Mpho, and I visiting Madiba and his wife Graça Machel at their home in Qunu, a few days before Christmas in 2005.

I REMEMBER that his welcoming voice came to us from an inner room before we saw him. 'So the professor has arrived! This is a special day for us.' There was banter in his voice. He came into view just as he was saying, 'The story of the professor's visit will be in all the newspapers! Qunu never gets visited by professors.' We all laughed: Madiba, Graça, Mpho and I.

I REMEMBER his banters. Tinged with kingly condescension, they were gifts to be savoured. They were a delicate ritual whose impact was heightened by his legendary memory for people's names. He relaxed you by banter, all the while conferring personal recognition. The combination of banter and recognition was powerful: it bound you to him. This was how he won millions of people over to him.

I REMEMBER at that evening's dinner before Christmas how Madiba's face seemed to radiate fulfilment. His elbows resting on the arms of his chair, hands clasped against his chest, he frequently scanned the room with his eyes. What he saw around the room were twenty smartly dressed grandchildren and great-grandchildren. Four generations of the Mandela family gathered in the room.

I REMEMBER the harsh glare of fluorescent lights was turned off, allowing candlelight and multi-coloured Christmas tree bulbs to give a soft glow of intimacy to the room. Madiba seemed to take it all in with an inner conversation, not conveying strong emotion but feeling it deeply. He would never tell what he felt. The movement of his face and his eyes, and his entire upright bearing, were his words.

I REMEMBER during that visit when he welcomed into his home four dignitaries of the Methodist Church of Southern Africa. As they walked in with a quiet dignity, Madiba said in welcome, 'The fact that people of your standing come to see us gives us the impression that we are not such irredeemable sinners.' Serious, complicated banter, inviting interpretation.

I REMEMBER that I joined Madiba and Graça in early January 2006 at their Maputo home where Madiba would sit with his legs stretched out in front of him across a leather leg rest. Graça offered us drinks. 'Another glass of water,' I responded. But Madiba answered: 'If you have Cuban rum you can send it.'

I REMEMBER Madiba at that moment recalling a story about Cuban rum. 'I once said that to a top leader of the West who did not like that joke.' 'Who was that?' I asked. 'Bush! He didn't like it. He said, "Will you drink something?" I said, "Yes please, Cuban rum!" He did not like that joke. Then I went to Cuba: straight from him to Cuba!'

I REMEMBER long quiet moments with Madiba when neither of us said anything. He appeared to be interviewing himself; seeming to grasp at flashes of memory as they passed by in his long life, and would suddenly tell a story. 'Queen Elizabeth says to me, "Nelson, when we are just talking privately in my office, just call me Elizabeth. Only when we are in a formal occasion must you refer to me as Your Majesty." So that's what we do.' Thus, he signified a special bond. I thought I spotted an intriguing innocence in a great man thrilled at having been confirmed a special friend of a great woman.

I REMEMBER Madiba telling one of his last stories with me. In this at his expense and others he told how when he was a boy herding cattle he saw some bees coming out of the ground. He went to investigate and found plenty of honeycombs. He took some home where, after everyone had enjoyed the honey, they began to quiz him about where exactly he found the honey. To their consternation, he told them the bees had made their home in a grave. Too late! Everyone had enjoyed the honey and probably lived long enough, like Madiba himself, to tell the story.

In Memoriam

Jakes Gerwel

He had a sense of collective leadership. He always raised the issue of how the individual relates to the collective leadership, how the individual's experience and conduct is influenced by the collective, and how it feeds back into the collective.

He had this uncanny ability to not just reflect but, as it were, 'forward-flect' on a decision.

He had this genuine belief — and he often argued with me about the provability of it — that human beings are essentially 'good-doing beings, beings who do good'.

He never expressed a word of bitterness. If he had bitterness, he worked with it; he internalised it, and buried it away. He would sometimes say to me, 'Some things are better not to dwell on.'

Mandela was so generous in his relationships with those who could be described as the adversary. If you talked about the enemy, which he didn't regard as an enemy, he would say, 'Be kind to your enemy; be kind to your adversary.'

I would say that the thing I remember him teaching me was: 'Jakes, never let your enemy choose the terrain of combat by reacting in anger. If you act in anger to anybody, even if it's your friend, you are allowing that person to choose the terrain.'

Madiba always used to say that every person wherever they find themselves is capable of being a leader.

Ahmed 'Kathy' Kathrada

I accompanied the president to Pretoria and as is his practice he informed his staff beforehand about what he wanted for supper or lunch. When we sat down at the table I found that he had ordered samp and beans, which was one of our favourite dishes in prison. He does not care very much for the exotic. His tastes are simple and straightforward.

He doesn't do anything in a hurry; he gives it a lot of thought.

There is an element of the aristocracy in him, but if anything I'd say he tended to be over democratic.

At ANC NEC meetings he would want to go out of his way to get the views of each person. It's laborious but he would do it.

It takes a lot to anger him. He is very very tolerant, very accommodating of views of people and their idiosyncrasies. But don't anger him to the extent where he can start disliking you because he is very very firm in his dislike.

Anything he undertakes he does with a degree of, you can almost call it fanaticism.

There have been occasions where he can be very firm and unyielding. It took all sorts of persuasion and pressures to get him to move on an issue.

Sifiso 'Selby' Masikane [as told by his daughter, Fikile Masikane]

My father would come home and share a joke or two that President Mandela, or as he called him uBaba, had shared with them. My aunt mentioned that my father said that even though Mr Mandela was funny he also had a strict side to him and that he was a no-nonsense man.

I remember when Mr Mandela flew the wives and children of his bodyguards to Mozambique to spend time with them because they had been away for a long time. During that trip I remember my father boasting about the perks of being a bodyguard for the head of state. Another perk was that we were able to enjoy Michael Jackson's South Africa concert with my parents.

Thobile 'Tall' Mtwazi

I remember hearing a thundering noise like a train on top of us. I thought a bomb had exploded. The chemist's front windows shattered and blew into the shop and medicines on the shelves flew all over the place. We grabbed the

Old Man and pulled him to the floor and fell over him, covering him with our bodies like a pack of cards.

Mary Mxadana

It's not nice to deal with a man of Mr Mandela's stature. It's difficult indeed because he's not only an ordinary president of a country, but he's the president of the world. A renowned leader so everyone wants to have his time.

The problem is that he is a people's person. He is very reluctant to let anyone down. It's in him; it's not something that he puts up. We are here to try and make him aware that he cannot cope.

I have to put myself in the boots of the people who would like to touch him, take a photo with him and at the same time I have to protect him.

If he had his way he would have liked to roam the streets as an ordinary person.

He loved to go home to Mthatha once in a while to see his home village.

You cannot stop children from coming to him and shaking his hands. Those are his basic wishes.

A three-year-old who saw him at Cosatu wanted to sing 'Nkosi Sikelel' iAfrika' for him and he listened, he didn't move. If the security car was waiting outside to move we knew that he would have preferred listening to the child and to be slightly late.

He sits and he meditates and he remembers things. If he has asked you to do something don't ever think he forgets.

Sometimes he relives the things that he would like to do in his quiet moments and if he remembers something and he has to talk to someone at that time he does that.

He is fanatical about time. Time is uppermost.

He expresses his wishes in a gentle and convincing way and it is very difficult to deny him some of his wishes except when they go against security rules and regulations.

He sleeps well, a maximum of five hours. At 5 am he is dressed and going for a walk.

He is religious about consultation.

He believes in human beings, in each and every person. He believes that each person has something to contribute. He doesn't do anything without consulting.

He doesn't have secrets. He doesn't have serious skeletons in the cupboard because he believes in approaching people and expressing his beliefs very openly.

John Reinders

He is a down-to-earth but a very firm man. If he wants something, he'll get it and his requests won't be unreasonable.

Protocol tried to persuade him to wear the traditional pin-striped trousers and short black jacket when meeting new ambassadors. He replied, 'Why? I think we have to adapt and have our own protocol.'

Walter Sisulu

When I met him for the first time, at once I had ideas — it was as if I was meeting a person I had been waiting for and from that time on it was building something. There can be no doubt that I did make a contribution in building him up. He shaped me and I shaped him.

When it is right he will fight. If he's fighting he'll win.

He's extreme in many things. When he doesn't like a thing, he doesn't like a thing.

He is very stubborn. Oh no doubt, very stubborn. He gets very angry when things are not done. He can repeat a lecture several times on discipline. He does get irritated by the executive coming late and then he makes a big issue.

Me in particular he likes to ring; he wakes me up. One o'clock, two o'clock, it doesn't matter, he'll wake me up. I realise that after he has woken me up, this thing is not so important. Well, we discuss it but it didn't really require that he wakes me up at that time.

Nelson is a very kind person, he is very warm.

The laughter he gives is an indication of what he is — he laughs heartily and then is suddenly serious. That is how he is.

He gets angry when things are not done. He can repeat a lecture several times on discipline.

Epilogue

Madiba – Poem of Gratitude

Let us be grateful for the carriers of the highest truth,
for they are driven by the heart and guided by the spirit,
They may fall, they do fail, but they rise above with will,
For truth is their message and freedom is their voice.

Let us remember the pioneers of change,
Braving the frontline with armours of courage and purpose,
They may tire, they do bleed, but they rise above with strength,
For loyalty is their essence and humanity their family.

Let us respect the teachers of life and sacred wisdom,
Pouring knowledge upon us from their roots in the heavens,
They may rest, they do die, but they rise above with humility,
For their values are within us and their light is what guides us.

Let us admire the radiant beacons of compassion,
Forever transforming the darkness of fear into the light of love,
They may hurt, they do break, but they rise above with faith,
For kindness is their song and harmony their rhythm.

Let us unite with the devoted leaders of our nations,
Weaving together cultures and colours of our people,
They may stray, they do wane, but they rise above with unity,
For oneness is their paint and humanity their canvas.

Let us follow the healers of struggle and division,
Paving the path of forgiveness and reconciliation,
They may neglect, they do forget, but they rise above with respect,
For acceptance is their mission and love their foundation.

Let us call upon our father Nelson Rolihlahla Mandela,
The warrior, teacher, beacon, leader and healer within us all,
Who balanced love, light and humility in the face of fear, doubt and hatred,
To let us live, let us be and let us free.

By Jay Naidoo, Shanti Naidoo Pagé and Sumedha Garg

Biographies

Goolam Aboobaker 77
Goolam Aboobaker worked in the Office of the President as a member of the Cabinet Secretariat from October 1994. He researched policy matters before Cabinet, prepared summaries and highlighted matters of concern.

Denise Abrahams 190
Denise Abrahams worked as a personal assistant to Nelson Mandela at the Nelson Mandela Foundation from 2001 to 2004.

Lawrence April 101
Lawrence April worked as a close protector for Nelson Mandela when he visited Cape Town from 1994 until 2009.

Ethel Arends 181
Ethel Arends started work at the Nelson Mandela Foundation in 1999 as one of the correspondence administrators. In 2006 she was promoted to the position of records management co-ordinator.

Tania Arrison 131
Tania Arrison worked in the Office of the President from 1994 to 1999 in public liaison, corporate services

and then as secretary in the director general's office. She worked as executive personal assistant at the Mandela Rhodes Foundation from 2003 to 2007 and then at the Nelson Mandela Foundation until 2009.

Tania Bagley 125
Tania Bagley worked in the Presidency from 1995 to 2000 as a ministerial typist and secretary to the director of public liaison, the late Mr Chris van der Walt.

Gert 'Barries' Barnard 133
Gert 'Barries' Barnard was a captain in the South African Police who worked as a close protection officer for Madiba from April 1994 until October 2002. During this time he also served as an operational planning manager in the Presidential Protection Unit.

Pam Barron 226
Pam Barron started at the Mandela Rhodes Foundation in 2007 as the executive assistant to Professor Jakes Gerwel, the chairman of the boards of the Nelson Mandela Foundation and the Mandela Rhodes Foundation. After his death in November 2012 she was the executive assistant to Prof Ndebele who succeeded him.

Lydia Bergström 182
Lydia Bergström worked as an office administrator for Mandela from 1999 when he stepped down as president and started the Nelson Mandela Foundation. She was responsible for setting up and managing his office and then managed his residences a few months later. She left in 2001.

Hein Bezuidenhout 66
Hein Bezuidenhout was privileged to be involved in the protection of the presidents of South Africa since 1984 including Nelson Mandela until his resignation in 2003.

Elzette Botha 123
Elzette Botha began working on the Presidential Protection Unit in 1994 as a bodyguard to Nelson Mandela. She left in 2001 when she moved to the Middle East.

Bakkies Breytenbach 154
Bakkies Breytenbach protected President FW de Klerk from 1989 to 1996 as a member of the South African Police's Presidential Protection Unit. He then protected Mandela and Deputy President Thabo Mbeki. In 2004 he headed the Counter Assault Team to assist in high-risk operations and was promoted to brigadier.

Julia Brown 217
Julia Brown started working in 2006 as the executive assistant in the office of the executive director of the Mandela Rhodes Foundation.

Dudu Buthelezi 179
Dudu Buthelezi worked at the Nelson Mandela Foundation from 1999 when it was based in Mr Mandela's house in Houghton, Johannesburg. Her work entailed taking care of Mr Mandela's guests and to prepare his office and his house.

Anton 'Kallie' Calitz 167
Anton 'Kallie' Calitz started his police career in 1987. He worked as a protection officer for Nelson Mandela

from 1996 to 1999 and as a planning officer until 2001, when he resigned to join the corporate security sector.

Tasneem Carrim 135
Tasneem Carrim worked in Nelson Mandela's communications research unit from 1994 until 1999.

Des Chetty 150
Des Chetty worked for the Presidential Protection Unit from 1995 to 1997 as a member of Nelson Mandela's close protection detail. He conducted site advance inspections nationally and internationally and planned motorcade movements and hotel assessments, among others. 'I was one of the foot soldiers,' he says.

Russel Christopher 52
Russel Christopher was the KwaZulu-Natal provincial head of the ANC's Department of Intelligence and Security (DIS) and protected Nelson Mandela on an *ad hoc* basis from 1991 to 1994.

Hermann 'Harry' Coetzee 147
Hermann 'Harry' Coetzee was a bodyguard for President FW de Klerk until 1995 when he completed a task force course and joined Nelson Mandela as a close protector. He stayed with him for the duration of his presidency.

Yoga Coopoo 223
Yoga Coopoo is a biokineticist and sports scientist who currently heads the department of sport and movement studies at the University of Johannesburg. His speciality is rehabilitation through exercise. He worked with Nelson Mandela for eighteen months

from March 2006 and travelled with him on occasion to Mozambique.

Achmat Dangor 173
Achmat Dangor, award-winning writer, activist and development expert, was head of the Kagiso Trust, Independent Development Trust, the Nelson Mandela Children's Fund from 1998, the Nelson Mandela Foundation and the Ford Foundation's Southern Africa office. He was also director of advocacy at UNAIDS. Now retired, he devotes himself to his writing.

Jill Daniels 106
Jill Daniels integrated into the South African Police Service as part of the ANC VIP protection team. In 1994 she was deployed to the Presidential Protection Unit, into the team of President Mandela. In 1996 she moved to Deputy President Thabo Mbeki's protection team.

Lee Davies 218
Lee Davies began his association with the Nelson Mandela Foundation in 2006 when he assisted on the Nelson Mandela Annual Lectures. He joined the staff fulltime in 2008 as a database administrator, and was promoted to communication systems co-ordinator in 2011.

Mothomang Diaho 225
Mothomang Diaho is a medical doctor who joined the Nelson Mandela Foundation in 2006 to run its Dialogue programme which included the Nelson Mandela Annual Lecture, HIV and Social Cohesion programmes and the Promise of Leadership. She left in 2009 but continued to consult for the Foundation until 2013.

Loïs Dippenaar 138
Loïs Dippenaar worked in the Office of the President from January 1994 to September 2000. Part of her role was to co-ordinate President Mandela's international schedule from 1998 and she accompanied him on a number of state visits. After his retirement she assisted with setting up his post-presidency office.

Joe Ditabo 194
Joe Ditabo was employed in 2000 by Ismail Ayob, Madiba's former lawyer, as a driver for the Nelson Mandela Foundation. He received a better offer in 2002 but was persuaded to stay on as an employee of the Nelson Mandela Foundation. Two years later he was promoted to facility supervisor.

Jessie Duarte 37
Jessie Duarte served as a special assistant to Nelson Mandela from 1990 to 1994.

Maeline Engelbrecht 144
Maeline Engelbrecht was the Nelson Mandela Children's Fund's donor relations manager from 1995 for eight years and then joined the Nelson Mandela Foundation as a consultant to the chief executive and later as external relations and governance manager until 2008. She travelled with Madiba on his fund-raising trips.

Fuad Floris 28
Fuad Floris worked in an ANC team set up to protect Nelson Mandela from 1990 when he visited the Western Cape, Northern Cape and Eastern Cape. He later accompanied Mandela on various overseas trips and

continued protecting him on an *ad hoc* basis after his retirement until about 2008.

Sumedha Garg 243
Sumedha Garg is a volunteer working at Eagle Valley Farm on education, creative arts and healing with children in Naledi village.

Florence Garishe 196
Florence Garishe began work as a temporary receptionist for the Nelson Mandela Foundation in 2002 when the office was being run from his home in 13th Avenue Houghton. She became the Foundation's permanent receptionist in 2007.

Jakes Gerwel 237
Jakes Gerwel (1946–2012) was the director general in President Mandela's office and later the chairman of both the Nelson Mandela Foundation and the Mandela Rhodes Foundation.

Yase Godlo 203
Yase Godlo joined the Nelson Mandela Foundation as a finance administrator in 2004. In 2008 he was promoted to project manager and in 2012 to Mandela Day manager.

Ryno Gouws 116
Ryno Gouws was part of the Presidential Protection Unit from June 1994 until 1997, when he resigned to further his career in the private sector.

Ella Govender 142
Ella Govender became Madiba's household manager in

Cape Town on 1 January 1995. After he retired she continued assisting at his home whenever he was in the city. During her annual leave she volunteered to work for him at his Transkei home and Madiba took care of her travel costs.

Ashwyn Govind 47
Ashwyn Govind first protected Mandela in 1991 when he was part of the ANC's security structure. In 1995 he was integrated into the South African Police Service's Presidential Protection Unit and worked with Mandela throughout his presidency. He resigned from the unit in 2001 with the rank of captain.

Jerome Hardenberg 112
Jerome Hardenberg from the SAPS worked as a close protector and planning officer for Madiba from 1994 until his term ended in 1999. He was responsible for planning Madiba's first two events as president-elect in Cape Town. His last trip with Madiba was to Morocco and the UAE in 2001.

Verne Harris 206
Verne Harris started doing projects for Madiba's office in 2001 and joined the staff of the Nelson Mandela Foundation in 2004 to set up the Centre of Memory, and became the director of archive and dialogue in 2015.

Sello Hatang 227
Sello Hatang joined the Nelson Mandela Foundation as head of communications in 2008. In 2013 he was appointed as chief executive.

Wayne Hendricks 152
Wayne Hendricks worked as a close protector for Nelson Mandela from 1995 to 2001.

Conroy Herandien 159
Conroy Herandien worked as a close protector to Nelson Mandela from 1996 to 1999. He continued in this role after Mandela retired as president and until 2007.

Willie Hofmeyr 48
Willie Hofmeyr was the main event organiser in the Western Cape for the United Democratic Front and then the ANC when Nelson Mandela was released from prison until 1994. His role included organising events and personally briefing him ahead of each event.

Piet Irvia 163
Piet Irvia was a policeman with the rank of inspector who worked as a close protector, convoy driver and personal driver for Madiba from the beginning of 1996 until May 2002.

Hayley Jacobs (née Lyners) 118
Hayley Jacobs (née Lyners) started working at the Office of the President in 1994 as secretary to the director general, Professor Jakes Gerwel. After Mandela retired she continued with Professor Gerwel when he was chair of the Nelson Mandela Foundation and the Mandela Rhodes Foundation.

Shaun Johnson 215
Shaun Johnson is the founding executive director of the Mandela Rhodes Foundation, which was established in

2003. In 2006 he was the CEO of the Nelson Mandela Foundation. He is an award-winning author and journalist.

Anthea Josias 208
Anthea Josias worked at the Nelson Mandela Foundation from 2004 to 2006 as a senior project officer in the Centre of Memory.

Ahmed 'Kathy' Kathrada 238
Ahmed 'Kathy' Kathrada (1929–2017) was sentenced to life imprisonment with Mandela in 1964, and he served as President Mandela's parliamentary counsellor from 1994 to 1999.

Shadrack Katuu 214
Shadrack Katuu worked in information systems at the Nelson Mandela Foundation, part time from 2005 and full time from 2006 until 2010 with time off to complete his PhD. He currently works at the International Atomic Energy Agency.

Meme Kgagara 197
Meme Kgagara worked as residence manager in Johannesburg for Nelson Mandela from 2002 until he passed away on 5 December 2013. She continued to work with Mrs Machel until October 2014.

Zelda la Grange 99
Zelda la Grange joined President Mandela's office as a senior ministerial typist in 1994. In 1997 she was promoted to one of his three private secretaries. When he retired in 1999, he took her with him. She was his

executive personal assistant and managed his private office until his death.

Poppy Lukhele 166
Poppy Lukhele was a sergeant in the South African Police Service when she started working with Madiba as a close protection officer in 1997 and remained with the team after his retirement until her resignation from the South African Police Service in 2003.

Mac Maharaj 17
Mac Maharaj spent twelve years in prison with Nelson Mandela on Robben Island. When Mandela became South Africa's first democratically elected president in 1994, he named Maharaj as his minister of Transport. They retained a close friendship until the end of Mandela's life in 2013.

Trevor Manuel 92
Trevor Manuel was an anti-apartheid activist who served as a Member of Parliament under President Nelson Mandela and from 1996 as his finance minister. He continued in that portfolio under President Thabo Mbeki after Madiba's term of office ended. At a stage, he was the world's longest serving finance minister.

Kerileng Marumo 231
Kerileng Marumo started working at the Nelson Mandela Foundation in 2009 as a finance officer and was promoted to accountant in 2012 and financial manager in 2015.

Barbara Masekela 74
Barbara Masekela is an educator and activist who lived in exile for twenty-two years. She has served as South Africa's ambassador to the United States, France and Unesco. She worked as head of staff in Nelson Mandela's office from 1990 until 1994.

Sifiso 'Selby' Masikane 239
Sifiso 'Selby' Masikane (1969–2017) was an Umkhonto weSizwe operative who served as a bodyguard for Nelson Mandela from 1992 to 1999.

Simon Mothibi Mathatho 94
Simon Mothibi Mathatho began protecting Nelson Mandela from the day he was inaugurated as President of South Africa until 1998.

Moeketsi D Matlabe 170
Moeketsi D Matlabe worked with Nelson Mandela as a close protector from 1997 to 2006 and as a team leader in the rank of captain from 2006 until 2008.

Thoko Mavuso 36
Thoko Mavuso was an operative for Umkhonto weSizwe, the armed wing of the African National Congress, before becoming a personal assistant to Nelson Mandela from 1991 until 2011.

Elaine McKay 201
Elaine McKay worked at the Nelson Mandela Foundation from 2003 as Programme Manager: HIV and AIDS. After the 46664 campaign was launched in November that year it became part of her portfolio. She left the NMF in 2007.

SR Moodley 62
SR Moodley worked in the Presidential Protection Service as a close protector to Nelson Mandela in the Western Cape from 1993. It became known as the Presidential Protection Unit in 1996. He remained in this role until 1999 when Mandela stepped down as President. He continues to serve in the SAPS.

Linga Moonsamy 80
Linga Moonsamy was an Umkhonto weSizwe operative who began working for Nelson Mandela as a bodyguard in 1994 and resigned in 1999 after Madiba stepped down as president.

Faizel Moosa 34
Faizel Moosa was in an ANC unit that provided protection in the Western Cape for Nelson Mandela, and other struggle leaders, after he was released in February 1990 until shortly after the elections in 1994. He is currently South Africa's ambassador to Qatar.

Shiraz Moosa 45
Shiraz Moosa began working as a bodyguard for Nelson Mandela after his release in 1990. He later became a joint unit commander with Hein Bezuidenhout of the Presidential Protection Unit in the Western Cape. He ended his duties in 1997.

Makano Morojele 199
Makano Morojele worked as Programme Manager: Education for the Nelson Mandela Foundation from March 2003 to October 2006. She developed and implemented its strategy for the Nelson Mandela Rural Schools Project.

Thobile 'Tall' Mtwazi 239
Thobile 'Tall' Mtwazi (1966–2004) served as a chief bodyguard of Nelson Mandela from 1993 to 1999.

Thembeka Mufamadi 178
Thembeka Mufamadi was seconded by the Human Sciences Research Council in mid-1999 as a researcher to assist President Mandela with his memoirs on his presidential years. This was as a result of her work on the life history of Raymond Mhlaba. She worked with Mandela until 2002.

Mary Mxadana 240
Mary Mxadana (1947–2002) served as Mandela's first presidential personal assistant.

Jay Naidoo 243
Jay Naidoo is the founding general secretary of the Congress of South African Trade Unions. He served in Nelson Mandela's Cabinet as the minister responsible for Reconstruction and Development and later Posts, Telecommunications and Broadcasting.

Priscilla Naidoo 87
Priscilla Naidoo was a public relations officer to President Nelson Mandela from 1994 to 1999. Among her highlights was chairing the historic joint press conference with him and President Bill Clinton in 1998. She is currently the Acting Chief Director: Protocol and Ceremonial in the Presidency, South Africa.

Vimla Naidoo 140
Vimla Naidoo's first job after university was at President

Nelson Mandela's office from 1995. She joined the Nelson Mandela Foundation in 2001. She remains personal assistant to Mrs Graça Machel.

Shanti Naidoo Pagé 243
Shanti Naidoo Pagé is a volunteer working at Eagle Valley Farm on education, creative arts and healing with children in Naledi village.

Shirley Naidu 176
Shirley Naidu worked as the manageress for Nelson Mandela's official residence in Cape Town. Her duties included shopping and cooking for Mandela and Mrs Machel and their family and guests.

Njabulo S Ndebele 233
Njabulo S Ndebele is an academic and renowned writer of fiction. He served Nelson Mandela from 2012 as the chairman of both the Nelson Mandela Foundation and the Mandela Rhodes Foundation.

Xoliswa Ndoyiya 56
Xoliswa Ndoyiya worked for Nelson Mandela as his personal chef at his home in Johannesburg from 1992 until he passed away in 2013.

Oupa Ngwenya 209
Oupa Ngwenya, the founding secretary general of the Forum of Black Journalists and a corporate strategist and writer, joined the Nelson Mandela Children's Fund in 2004 – first as a consultant corporate strategist and then as the full-time head of strategic corporate communications from 2010 until 2016.

Andile Ngxabani 24
Andile Ngxabani began protecting Madiba from April 1990 on his first visit to Mthatha since his release. He co-ordinated all of Madiba's visits around Transkei until he was transferred to Cape Town in 1998. Thereafter he was a security co-ordinator locally, nationally and internationally until Madiba stepped down as president in 1999.

Bob Nicholls 79
Bob Nicholls worked as a security advisor and instructor between 1992 and 1994, after which he was appointed as an international advisor to assist with the integration of all of the various VIP protection units, including those of the ANC and the police force.

Sam Nwamusi 70
Sam Nwamusi was an Umkhonto weSizwe operative who returned to South Africa in 1993 and led an underground team to provide assess protection at Nelson Mandela's rallies. After the country's first democratic elections he worked openly as a close protector to Mandela.

Boniswa Nyati 188
Boniswa Nyati began working at the Nelson Mandela Foundation in January 2000 to help respond to letters written to Mandela from supporters. She was later promoted to information resource officer and processed the gifts for Mandela and awards he received. She left the organisation in 2012.

Valene Peacock 229
Valene Peacock is a paramedic attached to the South African National Defence Force Presidential Medical

Unit, which takes care of former presidents and deputy presidents. She began working with Nelson Mandela in 2008 and finished at the end of 2009.

Sathie Pillay 60
Sathie Pillay worked with Nelson Mandela from early 1992 until 1997 when he was part of the VIP protection unit in KwaZulu-Natal. He drove the armoured vehicle and also worked as a bodyguard in the team.

Stephanus 'Fanie' Pretorius 90
Stephanus 'Fanie' Pretorius was a professional public servant who began serving President Mandela in 1994 as head of the Cabinet Secretariat but moved to the position of Chief Director: Corporate Services, which included all aspects of administration and the personnel and household staff of the president and deputy president.

Bridgette Prince 185
Bridgette Prince worked at the Nelson Mandela Foundation from 2000 until 2005 to manage its HIV programme. Her responsibilities included managing research projects and executing and communicating their outcomes. She also liaised with government and civil society stakeholders, including traditional leadership, educators and regional bodies.

Lucia Raadschelders 232
Lucia Raadschelders worked as an underground operative for the ANC in the 1980s and in 1994 she worked for the organisation in South Africa. She joined the staff of the Nelson Mandela Foundation as a photo archivist in 2010.

Moosa Ramjoo 76
Moosa Ramjoo joined Nelson Mandela's protection team in 1993 when he was campaigning for South Africa's first democratic elections. He continued working with him until 2000.

Neo Lekgotla laga Ramoupi 219
Neo Lekgotla laga Ramoupi started working at the Nelson Mandela Foundation as a senior project officer from October 2006 to May 2007.

Sunée Rautenbach 212
Sunée Rautenbach started working at the Nelson Mandela Foundation in 2004 as a human resources administrator. She was promoted to HR manager in 2007 and remained in this position until 2009 when she left to pursue other interests.

John Reinders 241
John Reinders (1951–2008) served as Mandela's chief of protocol throughout his presidency.

Wally Rhoode 40
Wally Rhoode was one of a small group of ANC MK cadres sent out of South Africa to train to be bodyguards for Nelson Mandela in 1990. He remained on his team until 1994.

Zanele Riba 73
Zanele Riba worked as an archivist at the headquarters of the African National Congress from August 1993 until February 2007. She joined the Nelson Mandela Foundation as an archivist in April 2007.

Lwaephe Selepe 192
Lwaephe Selepe is a paramedic attached to the South African National Defence Force Presidential Medical Unit, which takes care of former presidents and deputy presidents. He worked with Mandela from 2002 until 2009.

Sam Shitlabane 57
Sam Shitlabane was an Umkhonto weSizwe operative who in 1992 joined the ANC team to protect Nelson Mandela. He became a team leader of President Mandela's protection team and later national commander responsible for the teams in Cape Town and Pretoria.

Buyi Sishuba 187
Buyi Sishuba joined the Nelson Mandela Foundation in 2000 as a correspondence administrator. In 2011 she was promoted to the personal assistant of the chief executive officer of the Foundation.

Walter Sisulu 242
Walter Sisulu (1912–2003) was sentenced to life imprisonment with Mandela in 1964. He remained his closest confident and adviser.

Rory Steyn 107
Rory Steyn protected Madiba from the first to the last day of his presidency – 10 May 1994 to 16 June 1999. With the rank of lieutenant-colonel throughout, he started as unit commander of the Johannesburg Police VIP unit and transferred to the Presidential Protection Unit in January 1996.

Omar Suleman 53
Omar Suleman began protecting Nelson Mandela in 1992 as part of his work for the ANC's Department of Intelligence and Security. He continued in this role after his unit was integrated into the South African Police Service, until 1998.

Adrian Sydow 169
Adrian Sydow worked as a close protector of Mandela from 1996. After he was injured in a car accident en route to Mandela's house that year he was transferred to technical support where he did venue protection. He left in 1999.

Arch Sydow 50
Arch Sydow was part of an ANC unit that protected Nelson Mandela after his release in 1990 when he was in the Western Cape. He stopped protecting him in 1994.

Lolo Tabane 84
Lolo Tabane served as Director: Protocol and Ceremonial Services in the Presidency from 1994 to 1999.

Donny Thebus 95
Donny Thebus was a United Democratic Front activist who, on 11 August 1994, was amalgamated into the South African Police Service where he was deployed to President Mandela's security detail for the duration of his five years as head of state of the Republic of South Africa.

Tau Thekiso 165
Tau Thekiso first worked with Madiba from 1997 to 1999 as a planning officer for the Presidential Protection Unit, then as team leader from 1999 to 2001 and finally as the head of the Unit from 2004 to 2010.

Tony Trew 32
Tony Trew worked with Nelson Mandela at various times between 1990 and 1999. Among his roles was in the reception committee for the Wembley Concert in 1990 and from 1994 to 1999 in the communications unit in the Office of the President.

Jason Tshabalala 21
Jason Tshabalala, an Umkhonto weSizwe operative, began protecting Nelson Mandela on his visit to Lusaka in 1990 and was integrated into the South African Police Service in 1994. He built Mandela's protection structure in South Africa and later headed the Presidential Protection Unit. In 2005 he left to work for the Airports Company of South Africa.

Jan van der Walt 86
Jan van der Walt was a medic in the South African Military Health Service and he worked for Nelson Mandela from 1995 to 1999.

Etienne van Eck 129
Etienne van Eck, a police captain, jointly commanded Nelson Mandela's security from May 1994 in a newly formed unit of former South African Police and Umkhonto weSizwe soldiers. He held the rank of major when he last protected Mandela on 2 February 1996.

Henk van Heerden 157
Henk van Heerden worked in the Presidential Protection Unit from 1996 as a static shift commander and from 1997 in the Operational Planning and Technical Support Section. From 2004 at the Security

Advisory Service, he advised on security at President Mandela's Houghton and Mthatha residences until his passing on.

Lizanne van Oudtshoorn-Richle 103
Lizanne van Oudtshoorn-Richle worked for Nelson Mandela as Protocol Officer: Ceremonial Services at the Office of the President from 1994 to 1999.

Desmond van Rooyen 120
Desmond van Rooyen began protecting President Nelson Mandela from 1994 after he moved over from President de Klerk's security team. From 1999 he was a member of the PPU's operational planning section and later became the Pretoria commander involved in planning security for Mandela's daily movements and foreign visits.

Marieta van Wyk 97
Marieta van Wyk worked for four South African Presidents: PW Botha, FW de Klerk, Nelson Mandela and Thabo Mbeki in supply chain management and logistics. Professor Jakes Gerwel, the director general in President Mandela's office promoted her in 1997 to a director in the department. She retired in 2005.

Jeremy Vearey 26
Jeremy Vearey worked as a bodyguard for Madiba between December 1990 and January 1994 when he was a member of the Western Cape command structure of the ANC's Department of Intelligence and Security. He is currently a major general in the South African Police.

Marius Visser 127
Marius Visser worked as a plain-clothes police officer in President Mandela's Union Buildings office from 1994 to 1996.

Naomi Warren 221
Naomi Warren started working for the Nelson Mandela Foundation as a volunteer in 2006 in the HIV/AIDS programme. At the end of that year she became programme co-ordinator for the newly formed Dialogue Programme. From 2008 to 2010 she worked as the Dialogue Programme manager.